PRAISE FOR *THE ADVENTURE GA*

"One of 10 outdoor books that shaped the last decade."

—*Outside Magazine*, 2020

"In *The Adventure Gap*, James Edward Mills, an African American journalist who covers environmental issues and outdoor recreation, highlights the ancestral legacy shared between him and the Denali team . . . By the end of the book, whether or not the team reaches the summit becomes irrelevant; each team member returns to their respective community as leaders of their own expeditions, traversing a socio-economic crevasse to triumph at the summit."

—*Sierra Magazine*

"It seems to me that Mills has thrown down the gauntlet for those of us who love the wilderness. How will we promote outdoor adventure to people of color? How can we get more diverse people into the mountains? How can we protect the future of the lands that we love?"

—Jason D. Martin, The Alpine Institute

"In his experiences camping, hiking, and mountain climbing, Mills noticed that he was often the only African American participating in these activities. As he explains here, the outdoors community never made him feel unwelcome, but he became concerned that so few people of color were involved. He emphasizes the importance of encouraging youths from a variety of backgrounds to take part, not only to broaden their horizons but also to help protect the environment by raising a new generation of outdoor enthusiasts who will work to save it. He profiles six different people of color who are either currently involved in outdoor activities or have been historically significant. He intersperses these profiles with a description of Expedition Denali, a climbing trek composed of a group of people of color who, in 2013, attempted to summit America's highest peak, Alaska's Denali (also known as Mount McKinley). The author's description of the expedition is gripping, and these exciting segments are nicely balanced with the profiles, which give historical and cultural context to the goals of Expedition Denali. With journalistic clarity, Mills sheds light on a previously overlooked segment of history and culture."

—*School Library Journal*

"It's one thing to say the outdoors is for everyone—but it's also true that not everyone uses outdoor resources equally, for a variety of reasons: access, safety, feeling welcome, and more. Marginalized populations are much less likely to utilize wilderness spaces. Mills addresses these issues in this book, and also writes about the first all-African American climbing team to climb Denali, in Alaska. He writes about the journeys and accomplishments of the various members, shares his own story, and looks at how these stories are situated in our larger world."

—***Book Riot***

"As our country grows to be increasingly multi-cultural, it is vital that people of diverse racial and cultural groups develop a passion and love for the outdoors in order to protect and advocate for preservation of our wild places. *The Adventure Gap* provides an excellent introduction into what is needed to make this a reality."

—Susan Weida, Delaware Valley Appalachian Mountain Club

James Edward Mills
Foreword by Shelton Johnson

The Adventure Gap

Changing the Face of the Outdoors

10th Anniversary Edition

MOUNTAINEERS BOOKS

MOUNTAINEERS BOOKS is dedicated to the exploration, preservation, and enjoyment of outdoor and wilderness areas.

1001 SW Klickitat Way, Suite 201, Seattle, WA 98134
800-553-4453, www.mountaineersbooks.org

Printed in the United States of America

27 26 25 24   1 2 3 4 5

Cover design: Jen Grable & Ellis Failor-Rich
Design and layout: Kate Basart/unionpageworks.com

Map: Marge Mueller, Gray Mouse Graphics; base map provided courtesy of National Outdoor Leadership School (NOLS)

Cover photograph: *Billy Long at 11,000 feet on Denali* (courtesy of Hudson Henry)
Back cover photographs: *Woman walking with children* (courtesy of NOLS/Brad Christensen); *Erica Wynn* (courtesy of Hudson Henry)

Library of Congress Cataloging-in-Publication Data is on file for this title at https://lccn.loc.gov/2024005392. An ebook record is available at https://lccn.loc.gov/2024005393.

Printed on recycled paper

ISBN (paperback): 978-1-68051-680-7
ISBN (ebook): 978-1-68051-681-4

MIX
Paper from responsible sources
FSC® C008955
FSC www.fsc.org

An independent nonprofit publisher since 1960

To Rubye and Billy, for making the sacrifices and enduring the struggles of your time so that I could always pursue my dreams—no matter how foolish or frivolous. Thank you, Mom and Dad.

To Shamane—after 25 years of marriage, your love and support have made possible every adventure. I am who I am because of you.

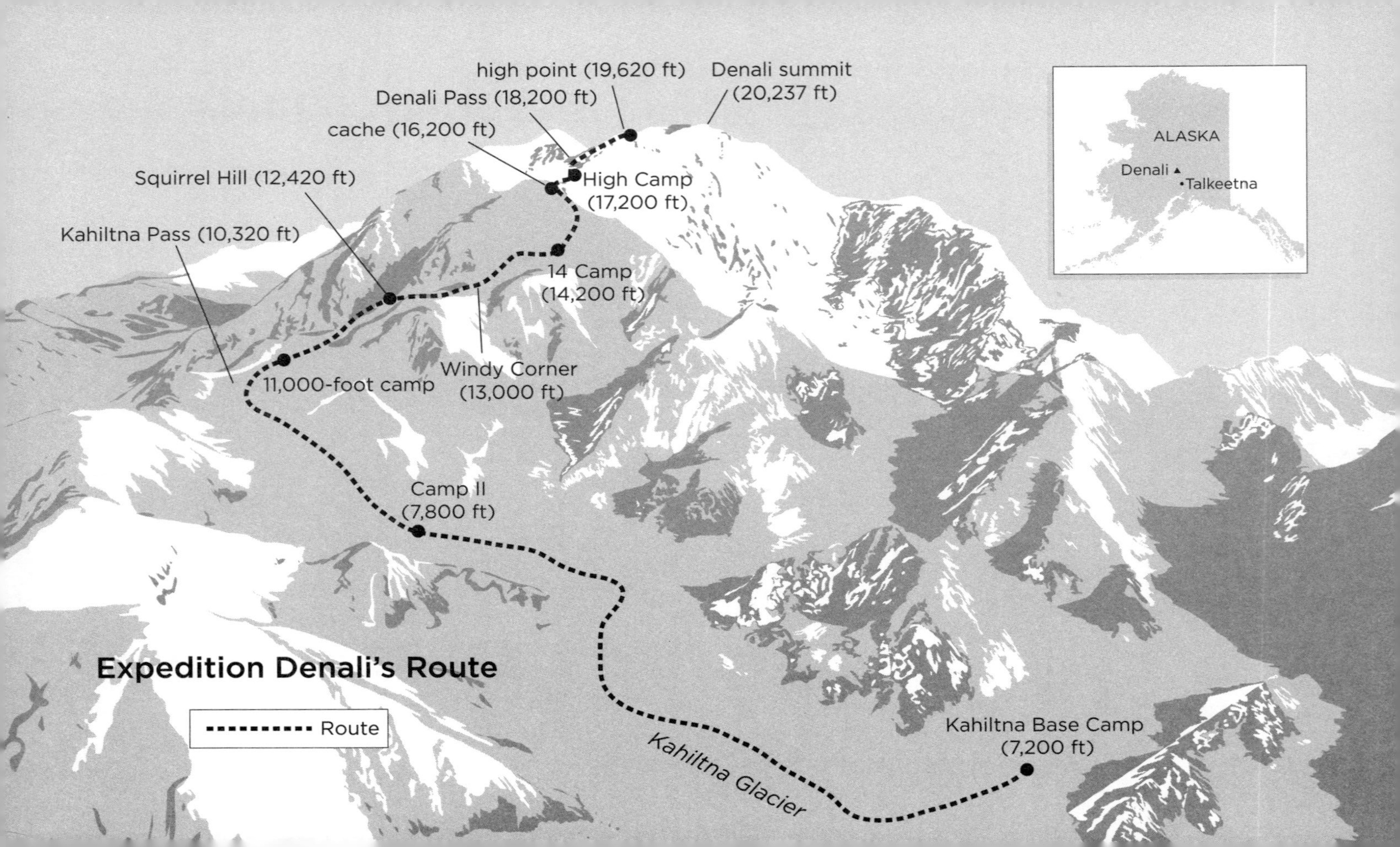
Expedition Denali's Route
Route
high point (19,620 ft)
Denali summit (20,237 ft)
Denali Pass (18,200 ft)
cache (16,200 ft)
High Camp (17,200 ft)
Squirrel Hill (12,420 ft)
Kahiltna Pass (10,320 ft)
14 Camp (14,200 ft)
Windy Corner (13,000 ft)
11,000-foot camp
Camp II (7,800 ft)
Kahiltna Glacier
Kahiltna Base Camp (7,200 ft)
ALASKA
Denali
Talkeetna

Contents

Foreword

As a kid growing up in Detroit, I knew about Althea Gibson, Muhammad Ali, Wilt Chamberlain, Wilma Rudolph, Willie Mays, and Jesse Owens. But I never heard anything about Charlie Crenchaw. He was a pioneer in a sport that none of my childhood friends ever talked about: mountain climbing.

As children we never saw African-Americans in the movies climbing mountains; we saw Clint Eastwood in The Eiger Sanction. Yet had I known then what I know now, I would've been upset that the lead character was played by Eastwood and not by Jim Brown! There were African-American alpinists at the time, but you wouldn't have known it unless you were one of them.

It's obvious that we can be influenced by who we see in the media and what we see them doing on screen and in print. But impressionable youth can also be shaped by what they don't see African-Americans doing much of, including kayaking, backpacking, skiing, mountain biking, horseback riding, and mountain climbing.

I went on to become a park service ranger, but it wasn't because there were role models for me when I was a child. Robert Stanton, who would eventually become the first African-American director of the National Park Service, was already a park ranger when I was still young, but no one ever told me about him at the time, and I never read about him in a newspaper, a magazine, or saw him on television. And that's a shame. Stanton broke through barriers as the first Black director of our national parks, and more of our youth should be aware of his great accomplishment.

This is why James Mills's *The Adventure Gap* is such an important book. Besides being well written, insightful, dramatic, and often lyrical, it's also essential reading for anyone who desires a more complete vision of who is experiencing the Great Outdoors and the achievements of African-Americans historically and today. The wilderness experience shaped the American character, and Africans in America were an integral part of that national story.

Many people today have heard of Jedediah Smith and Jim Bridger; they were Euro-American trappers who have since attained legendary status. But during that same time period, there were also African-American mountain men like James P. Beckworth and Edward Rose. Unfortunately, Beckworth and Rose never became part of popular culture. If they had, perhaps more African-American kids today would be inspired to follow in their footsteps and explore the deserts, plains, grasslands, and mountains that constitute a collective heritage that is as much African as it is European.

The Adventure Gap tells the story of Expedition Denali, a unique all African-American mountaineering team, of which young people of every background should be aware. The team's members pushed themselves physically, emotionally, and spiritually to achieve something not for just themselves, but for all of us. Through their act we see that public lands and wilderness belong to *all* Americans. Their ascent of the highest peak in North America makes the statement that "the pursuit of happiness," for a people brought to these shores in bondage, must of necessity lead to a mountaintop.

In the late 1960s, Dr. Martin Luther King, Jr., spoke metaphorically about his own journey to the mountaintop and his vision of the

Promised Land. Anyone who has stood at the rim of the Grand Canyon, or on top of Half Dome in Yosemite Valley, or on the lip of the Upper Geyser Basin in Yellowstone, has seen a view as real, and as sublime, as any in this world. When we as African-Americans explore deep caverns, or raft wild rivers, or climb big mountains, we extend the Civil Rights Movement vertically and horizontally to encompass all that's wild in America. And we claim our full inheritance as citizens of this country. We are saying that *we* are Americans.

James's book is not simply a chronicle of an expedition to the top of Denali, it's an account of a door being pushed open that had been locked shut and barricaded. The wind blowing through that doorway has the sweetness of mountains about it, but it is cold. The night is upon us, but the stars will light the way. Take their hands. Hold on to Erica, Shobe, Billy, Scott, Adina, Tyrhee, DeBerry, Ryan, Rosemary, the other courageous members of Expedition Denali, and James, who brought their story to us.

Together we will all climb that high peak. Together we will find the Promised Land.

—Shelton Johnson
Mariposa, California
June 2014

Prologue

Mount Baker

Mount Baker, Washington, August 13, 2012

It was two o'clock in the afternoon on a beautiful summer's day. Exhausted, I slept in a crumpled heap as warm rays of sunlight shone through the open door and gently swept away the chill of a mountainside covered in ice and snow.

"You were just lying there in your tent, outside your sleeping bag, fully clothed facedown like you were dead!" laughed Adina Scott. "You even still had your boots on!"

Our team had just summited Mount Baker. And it was true, I was totally wiped out after the long walk back across the Easton Glacier. Once inside our base camp perimeter, safe from the risk of a crevasse fall, I had dropped my pack, untied my rope, and helped to stow away the group gear. I had somehow managed to get my crampons off, letting them fall beside my ice ax and helmet in a pile of snow. Then I had crawled inside my tent and collapsed into a deep, deep sleep. That evening, over a sparse meal of rehydrated beans and makeshift quesadillas, my teammates enjoyed a good laugh at my expense.

I laughed right along with them; I couldn't help it, even though the climb had in fact taken quite a toll. I felt totally spent, beaten near to death. Even as a climber with more than a few years of mountaineering under my belt, I could not remember the last time I had ever felt so physically wiped out. But if my fellow climbers could have seen my face buried under the nylon folds of my down jacket as I slept, they would have seen that I was smiling. Despite the pain I felt in my aching joints, I enjoyed a feeling of supreme satisfaction. Having gotten up well before dawn to scramble over acres of rock and ice and pushing myself harder than ever before, I was on the path of something truly wonderful. And yet even then, despite my efforts to get this far, deep inside I knew my role as a climber on this team was coming to an end.

In camp that evening, I thought back to three days earlier. Straining against the weight of our heavy packs, we had hiked in along a dirt trail lined with trees and scattered with pine needles. Was it really just three days ago? As always happens in climbing, time on the mountain intensifies, and I felt that I had been immersed in this adventure for much longer. For the summit bid, we were thirteen members in all, in two teams. Seven were students of the National Outdoor Leadership School (NOLS), there to learn, with two instructors to guide us on a roped ascent of Mount Baker, the second most glaciated mountain in the United States outside of Alaska. The other four, NOLS instructors as well, came as a media team, armed with cameras and microphones to document our climb as we aimed to make history.

Climbing Mount Baker was the second of several training missions to put the first majority team of African-Americans on the summit of the highest peak in North America, an ambitious project called "Expedition Denali." In a world where far too few people of color spend time recreating outdoors, our mission was to demonstrate that, despite all evidence to the contrary, Black folks do indeed climb.

Though I was immensely proud to be in the group and committed to doing my part, on this trip I was also struggling. Growing up, I had successfully climbed several of the high peaks in the San Gabriel and San Bernardino mountains near my childhood home in Los Angeles, and I had climbed a few routes of vertical rock in Yosemite in 2005 and

2006. My climbing days since then had been few and far between. My last effort was in 2010, when I tagged along with professional climber Majka Burhardt to Ethiopia where I helped her set up a series of small scrambles on the Gheralta Massif near the village of Tigray.

Over the years, as a professional journalist, I have interviewed several leading alpinists such as Ed Viesturs, Peter Athans, Steve House, and Hilaree O'Neill. I have gotten to know big name rock climbers Lynn Hill, Ron Kauk, Alex Honnold, and Tommy Caldwell. And I've met Royal Robbins and Yvon Chouinard, living legends in mountaineering. For the past twenty years, I had been a tangential part of the climbing community, but with few notable accomplishments of my own.

At the ripe old age of forty-six, the challenges I faced on Mount Baker had nothing to do with my race but everything to do with the simple fact that I was out of shape. On the first day, even as we sucked down the relatively rich air just a few thousand feet above sea level, it was clear that I was out of my depth. I had started to lag behind as we climbed slowly above the tree line and onto the first of several snowfields.

Wearing a new pair of boots, I realized, was a rookie move, and my feet were now plagued with blisters, two of them the size of silver dollars; an old injury from a fall twenty years earlier nagged my left hip, causing me to limp. I could do nothing but endure the pain as we kicked steps into the trail ahead. The path was slippery with a combination of ankle-deep snow and bare rocky ground, which made it that much harder to carry fifty pounds of personal gear, climbing equipment, and food on my back. I'd studied the maps, and I knew we had miles to go before we'd reach the Easton Glacier and the spot 8,000 feet above sea level that would serve as our first camp.

From the moment I had heard about Expedition Denali, I was determined to be a part of it, including this training climb of Mount

Baker. But on a rest break, as I sat panting and drenched in sweat, I wondered whether I was in over my head. As if on cue, one of the strongest members of our team came up to me and asked, "You want us to take some of your weight?" I knew then that I was not alone in that wondering.

Adina moves over mountain terrain like an elfin princess right out of Tolkien. I must outweigh her by forty pounds, but this thirty-two-year-old doctor of engineering has the carrying capacity and dexterity of a Peruvian llama. I reluctantly handed over a snow picket and an avalanche probe from the group gear I carried. They weren't the heaviest items in my pack by any means, but giving them up was a formal concession of my inability to carry my fair share as part of the team. The symbolism wasn't wasted on me. I had to do better.

As I trudged farther up the snowfield, each step was like taking a blow to the shins with a two-by-four. Every ten paces or so I'd stop, lean into my trekking poles, and take a dozen deep breaths. The rest of the team was out of sight over the next ridge as I plodded along, alone in the mountain wilderness. By this time we were well above tree line, and I found myself surrounded by a glaring landscape of white snow set against a crystal-blue sky. Slabs of bare granite poked through to reveal sparse patches of vegetation defying the ice that lingered despite the summer season. Sweat poured into my eyes and the sting of perspiration made it difficult to see—and nearly impossible to appreciate—the beauty all around me.

Eventually I caught up to one of the NOLS instructors, who asked if I'd had anything to eat. When I answered no, he made me take off my pack and choke down some food and water. I should know better, I told myself. I have to keep refueling. I was more out of practice than I'd realized.

We sat there chatting while I ate and drank. I was grateful for the distraction of conversation and the comfort of compassion. I could feel my strength slowly rebounding when our course leader Angela Patnode came back over the ridge, retracing her steps through the snow. "We're setting up camp over there," she said, pointing with a thumb over her shoulder. "I'm going to take your pack."

It would have been foolish to say no. She'd already dropped her pack at camp, so I transferred my own to her back and followed as she ascended the ridge. After scrambling over a rocky outcropping, we found ourselves in a big patch of open ground at the very edge of the glacier. Pockets of heather and wildflowers colored the landscape with splashes of green, yellow, and purple, throwing into contrast the white background of our objective, a maze of crevasses and ice walls at the base of Mount Baker.

Up ahead, I could see the rest of our team setting up tents and making camp. Angela handed me back my pack. A life coach from Montana, she was sensitive to the delicate psychology of failure. With my burden of weight, she passed back to me the dignity of walking the final steps to Crag View under my own power. Once again, the message was clear—I had to do better.

MOUNTAINEERING IS PERHAPS LIFE'S GREATEST METAPHOR. AS WE overcome the physical obstacles of dangerously low temperatures and high altitude, we not only push past our own physical limits but redefine the way we relate to the world and gain along the way a deeper understanding of ourselves. Mountains are like a three-dimensional relief map of the human spirit that illustrates the heights of our aspirations and depths of our despair. As we travel into them, struggling through the uncertain ether of danger and enduring the cold and limb-numbing fatigue, we can't help but reflect on our lives, the decisions we've made, and where we might be today if we'd taken a different path.

The mountain experience affects not only our reflections on the past, but also influences the way we think about the future. It allows us to realign our priorities and consider life from a new perspective. And even though this is a story based in fact, there's a spiritual transformation that occurs between fantasy and reality that lies at the very heart of every adventure.

At 20,237 feet above sea level, Denali, formerly called Mount McKinley, is the loftiest perch in the United States. As one of the so-called Seven Summits—the tallest peak on each continent—Denali is a much-valued prize on most climbers' bucket lists. Both physically and metaphorically: if you can succeed on Denali, you can likely succeed anywhere.

By summiting this high mountain, the members of the Expedition Denali team wanted to show that people of color—African-Americans in particular—do in fact have a place in outdoor recreation. The objective was to inspire a new generation of minority youth to seek out and enjoy a relationship with the natural world where they might come to play, pursue career opportunities, and fight for its long-term preservation. Like most climbing expeditions, the summit was not the sole goal. And for this expedition in particular, the ascent to the summit would be only the first step. The journey would continue for climbers back home in their communities, where each team member would be responsible for sharing their experience and offering encouragement to those around them who aspire to a life of adventure.

For these noble intentions, I wanted to be part of Expedition Denali, but my interest in mountaineering was indeed no more selfless than that of any other climber who ever lived. I wanted to join because I love the sport of climbing, the physical exertion, the view from the summit, and that sense of accomplishment that comes only from achieving a high peak. These self-serving human motives are typical of those who risk alienating friends, family, and fortune to become, as the writer Lionel Terray describes in his book of the same title, a "conquistador of the useless." Climbing is a pastime available primarily to those with the disposable income and leisure time to squander on an activity that has virtually no socially redeeming qualities. That's probably why I, along with many other men and women around the world, enjoy it so much. Climbing is the very definition of freedom.

My interest in climbing is also professional. As an outdoor journalist, I enjoy traveling to distant places to tell the stories of others in pursuit of their dreams. I like discovering what motivates climbers to do the things they do, and I want to encourage those who read my work to achieve audacious goals of their own. Yet in recent years I had felt my personal life falling short of the spirit of adventure I aimed to inspire in others. That persistent pain in my left hip had curtailed my physical activity, and I needed a physical challenge of consequence to aspire to, something that truly mattered. Expedition Denali sounded like just the thing. Still, climbing the highest peak in North America was only part of my objective.

My bigger goal was to better understand why so few people who look like me—African-Americans—seek out adventure in the natural world, whether by striding along a forest trail or tramping up an icy glacier. To tell that story well, I also needed to test myself. Although I'd spent plenty of time in the outdoors, it's one thing to "get away from it all" and quite another to press the boundaries of your soul and resist what ten million years of evolution have taught you to fear—hunger, cold, isolation, falling—by climbing a big peak. I believe we experience genuine freedom when we make a conscious choice to set aside the comforts of warmth, family, and financial security just to climb to a high place and enjoy the view of a distant horizon. Though we live in a nation whose founding principle is freedom, far too many of us deprive ourselves of the opportunity to get beyond our daily urban routine to gaze upon the grandeur of the natural world. And too many of us depriving ourselves of nature are people of color.

TWO DAYS AFTER MY INITIAL POOR PERFORMANCE, I FELT A GREAT deal stronger. It was the day before our summit bid, and I woke up feeling ready to go. Applying the lessons I'd learned about the importance of balancing rest with plenty of food and water, I began our ascent to our next bivy, a flat expanse of ice at the base of Mount Baker, on a full stomach. Earlier that morning, I'd polished off a full breakfast of pancakes slathered in a syrupy mixture of brown sugar melted with thick gobs of butter and washed down with rich hot chocolate. Weighed down with three liters of drinking water, I humped the load feeling lighter on my feet—with the full confidence that this time, I wouldn't bonk. And indeed, once I got going, I noticed that my pace had improved dramatically. The long steep climb up the snow-covered glacier held the combined challenge and advantage of a path carved by my teammates' boots, plunged deep into the snow, one after the other.

"Just swing your leg with the momentum of your boot and plant it. Shift your weight over your foot and rest," Adina said. "Take your next step and don't apologize to anyone for your pace."

Raised in the Pacific Northwest, Adina was thoroughly at home in the Cascade Mountains. She learned the art of glacier travel at a young age from her father, now a professor emeritus of mathematics at the University of Washington in Tacoma. Decades before, he had ventured west from his home in Philadelphia and fallen in love with the high mountains, later instilling in his children a strong appreciation for the outdoors and wonders of nature. Adina was a strong and able mountaineer. Despite the heavy load of her pack and the rough terrain, she moved with a grace and ease I admired. Perhaps for the first time, I recognized the value of gaining a talented mentor to help guide my own practice in climbing. Despite my years of experience on the mountains, as I watched Adina move and make decisions, I realized that I still had a lot to learn.

Up and along the upper edge of the glacier, we marched with a steady rhythm choreographed to each intake of breath and each beat of our hearts. Though we were roped together in teams of three, we moved as one, united in our objective to reach the summit.

"You're doing much better today," Angela told me when we stopped for a rest. "How do you feel?"

"Good," I replied. "It helps to have my tanks full. I feel stupid for not eating the other day."

She smiled sardonically with a nod that said, "No shit, knucklehead!"

AFTER DINNER, AS EVENING SLOWLY FELL OVER OUR CAMP, WE GATHered as a team. The plan was to head out well before dawn the following morning to make our bid for the summit. When our departure time was announced—3:00 A.M.!—the others probably shared my first thought: "Are you friggin' kiddin' me?"

But no one said anything. We just agreed to be roped up and ready to go. One by one we shuffled off to bed, each of us mentally preparing to roll out of camp in what many of us would still consider the middle of the night.

Hours later, I lay in my tent, still wide-awake, huddled against the cold. I was shivering, but only in part as a result of the temperature.

After all, in midsummer the predawn chill was well above freezing. I shook as much in nervous anticipation of what lay ahead. Around 1:30 in the morning, I crawled out of my sleeping bag to pee. Since my alarm was set for 2:00, I decided not to go back to sleep and instead passed the time firing up the stove to melt snow into drinking water. Others roused themselves slowly, fighting to get their bodies moving after too little sleep, and started making their own breakfast. By the light of headlamps in the otherwise total darkness, we put on our gear, complete with crampons and ice axes. Shortly after the appointed hour, we marched out of camp in rope teams of three.

As we walked through the night up the Easton Glacier, my headlamp restricted my field of vision to a bright white cone of light. Overnight the summer slush farther up the mountain had frozen to hard and slippery ice. The sharp spikes of our crampons were the only thing keeping us from losing our footing and then sliding down the mountain, past our base camp, and all the way back to Crag View. As I walked steadily forward, my worldview comprised nothing more than a coil of rope, the toes of my boots, and the gray-blue footprints of the climbers on lead ahead of me. As I plodded on through the darkness, nothing else mattered but the satisfying "snick" that sounded each time I kicked steel into snow.

It was a walk of faith—and one that demanded my full concentration. Despite the light from our headlamps, Billy Long and Tyrhee Moore, the other two members of my rope team, were all but invisible. Last in line, I used the rope to pace myself, walking just fast enough to keep the rope slack, but careful not to step on it; I also had to be careful not to let it pull tight and throw the men in front of me off balance.

Tyrhee was a college freshman from Washington, DC. With infectious enthusiasm and boundless energy, he epitomized our mission. By training young people like Tyrhee, who would in turn encourage his peers to embrace his passions, we all hoped that Expedition Denali would inspire thousands of young people just like him.

"Summit Team yellow!" I yelled. This was the code for our unit to slow down whenever any of us reached a switchback turn. Changing my ice ax to my uphill hand, I kick-stepped my way around it. "Summit Team clear!" I called when I was safely around the bend. I was doing better.

Around 5:00 A.M., two hours into our hike, we entered a treacherous field of cracks that could swallow a person whole. Without the benefit of full daylight, it was impossible to see the crevasses clearly. On lead, in front of all the rope teams, Angela carefully probed the snow for any dangerous spots in the path before her. By checking with her axe for a solid surface beneath the snow and ice before every step, she ensured the safety of the entire team. It made for slow going, but it was far better than the alternative. As Angela found and stepped over each small, traversable crevasse, she issued a warning shouted over her shoulder, alerting everyone to watch their step. My heart pounded as I carefully negotiated each deep fissure that split the glacier. Although most were only about 18 inches wide, every crack opened like a gaping black maw and seemed to suck down the light from my headlamp, disappearing to infinity. As I straddled each one, I compulsively tightened my grip on my ax, ever ready to arrest a fall should it come.

A few months earlier, marching across the Matanuska Glacier in the Chugach Range of Alaska on our first significant training session, our team hadn't been so lucky. We'd already been in the Chugach for ten days when we set off in our snowshoes toward our next campsite, linked together in four four-person rope teams. Under an overcast sky with low visibility, the terrain consisted of little more than a vast monochromatic snowfield. The only distinguishing feature was the dark forms of our team, highlighted by flashes of pigment from the bright clothing, backpacks, and the ropes that bound us together. With virtually no scenery to enjoy, the walking was profoundly monotonous, and we were all lost in our own thoughts when someone suddenly yelled, "Falling!"

Without looking back, I braced myself for a tug on my rope that never came. All three of my teammates were accounted for. Relieved that my team was okay, I turned to check on the two teams in the rear. One remained standing, four dark silhouettes against a white backdrop. But three members of the second team lay facedown in the snow, leaning heavily on their ice axes as an unseen weight pulled taut the ropes secured to their harnesses. The fourth member of their rope team, Alex Straus, was simply gone, dangling with a sixty-five-pound pack inside a crevasse of unknown depth.

Alex was one of several other students in the same NOLS mountaineering course that was training members of Expedition Denali. Even though nine other climbers, including me, had already passed over the spot where Alex fell, for some unknown reason the thin ice bridge that covered the crevasse collapsed under his weight. Fortunately, having trained for just such an emergency, the three remaining members of his rope team saved him from falling out of reach.

To avoid risking another fall, the other student climbers stayed put while one of the instructors built a rescue system of ropes and carabiners and safely hauled Alex out of the hole, a bit shaken but unharmed. After a few kind words of encouragement from our leaders, the rope teams fell back into line, and we continued toward our next camp on the Matanuska Glacier as if nothing had happened.

Months later, we cleared the crevasse field below the summit of Mount Baker without incident, to continue along a frozen passage that grew brighter as the sun rose behind us. We marched onward over increasingly steep terrain as dawn unfolded all around us. Until all at once, we stopped.

A long line of climbers intersected our path from the opposite direction, using a route from the west that was popular with commercial guides on Mount Baker. A stream of twenty clients roped into teams of six trudged steadily up to the base of the headwall, the steepest part of the climb. At the head of our rope team, Tyrhee gave way to the oncoming crowd, much to the consternation of Stephen Shobe, the oldest and most experienced member of our group. Given our fewer numbers and greater speed, it was frustrating to grind to a halt with our goal within view.

As I watched the party go by, I couldn't help but notice the broad array of ages, gender, relative fitness, and technical ability in their group. I imagined that they were all strangers to each other, and I couldn't help but compare their experience to ours. Surely they would make it to the summit, but each would likely experience it as an individual accomplishment. We, however, had climbed and would summit as a team, committed to a common purpose.

Here on Mount Baker, the experience of being part of a team had opened my eyes to the physical challenges that lay ahead on Denali. But it also yielded a better understanding of what it meant to work cooperatively toward a shared goal. Though our objective was the top of a high mountain, our mission was to demonstrate that anyone—regardless of race, ethnicity, gender, or disability—can share in the satisfaction of climbing. By operating as a team, any summit—any goal—is achievable.

Once the other group had cleared the headwall, we began our slow ascent along a narrow trail of switchbacks. Here for the first time we were fully exposed to the possibility of a longer and more dangerous fall should anyone slip. Though the view of the valley below was breathtaking, I kept my vision focused on the path in front of me, careful to keep pace with Tyrhee and Billy and mindful of the rope and the distance between us. Our crampons clicked against jagged rocks poking up here and there through the snow, threatening to catch a spike and trip us up. Then suddenly our heads cleared the height of the headwall to reveal a flat expanse leading up to a granite dome.

We stood in the middle of a saddle where several trails up the mountain converged. I could see yet another group of climbers in the distance making their way toward the summit. The sun shone down, providing actual warmth for the first time that day, and a gentle breeze stirred the air around us. We watched as the other climbers reached the summit and took pictures. A few minutes later they came down, smiling and clutching their cameras.

When the summit was at last clear, we made our way along the wide path to the peak. Each member of our party belayed the next to safety until all nine of us stood side by side on the volcanic dome. The morning sun warmed our faces as we gazed out over the Cascade Mountains and a sea of snowcapped peaks. We were still catching our breath, immersed in thought, when Adina pulled off her Gore-Tex shell. Underneath she wore a silver-sequined tank top over her down jacket.

"Am I the only one who brought summit bling?" she asked. We erupted in a chorus of cheers, high-fives, and adrenaline-fueled laughter. The wind howled with us as a sudden gust swirled around our dancing, crampon-clad feet.

FOR ALMOST TWO YEARS BEFORE THE PLANNED 2013 DENALI CLIMB, NOLS put together these mountaineering missions to train and build the team that would ultimately attempt this biggest North American summit. NOLS had reached out to organizations around the country to find participants willing to join this ambitious project to bring more people of color into the outdoors. I was one of many who answered the call, and a few months before our trips into the Chugach and Cascade ranges, seventeen of us interested in Expedition Denali gathered for the first time at a mountain cabin in Lake Tahoe, California.

By 2009, I had produced a short documentary on diversity in outdoor recreation for the Public Radio International program To The Best of Our Knowledge. I'd already written several magazine articles on the issue and was in the process of writing another, specifically about diversity in the national park system, when I took my first NOLS course through the Wind River Range of Wyoming. That was when I first met NOLS's newly hired diversity and inclusion manager, Aparna Rajagopal-Durbin. It was her idea to put together an all African-American team for a high-profile expedition to the summit of Denali. When the time came to choose the team, she invited climbers who were also leaders of organizations committed to helping spread the message of diversity. As a journalist who'd written about diversity in outdoor recreation, I was part of that list.

We were told from the outset that there would only be nine slots on the Denali summit team—so we knew that not all of us would be going to Alaska.

Our first fitness workout in Lake Tahoe, composed of multiple rounds of calisthenics meant to boost our metabolic output, had caused a few to disqualify themselves. Three more fell away after we had spent two weeks training on the Matanuska Glacier where Alex fell into the crevasse. Another few dropped out due to family or professional obligations or simply the inability to commit so much time and energy to training. The final nine who remained—myself included—trained for the Denali climb as a team, each wanting to prove ourselves worthy of the mission. Mount Baker was the final test before Expedition Denali officially got under way just nine months later.

The final list of Denali climbers would include only those who made it to the summit of Mount Baker. Technically that included me. But with a mountain twice as high looming in the future, the climbers had to do more than just reach the Baker summit. They had to excel getting there. To achieve the summit on a climb where the price of failure could mean death, everyone needed to be capable of pulling their weight and making sacrifices when needed. Though it was crushing to admit it, after Mount Baker, I knew I was the weakest link. I might have been able to climb past my obvious physical limitations, but I had no business being on the summit team and potentially putting others at risk.

Fortunately, the decision to quit was no longer mine to make. Two days after summiting Mount Baker, the team traveled back to the NOLS base in Conway, Washington, where the course instructors evaluated everyone's performance. And that's when they gave me the news. Although I had made it to the top of Mount Baker, my fitness level, as well as the apparent pain I experienced while carrying heavy loads, made me a liability.

"You did very well," Angela told me. "You really improved a lot after that first day, and you put in a lot of effort to make it to the summit. We were all impressed. But there's something you need to understand. We don't think you're ready for Denali."

I knew it was coming, so the news was less of a blow to my ego than it might have been. When you put into perspective what it means to climb any mountain, I think it's critical to clearly understand your motivation. Personally, I wasn't interested in putting my life or the lives of my team on the line just to see the view from a high peak. I can appreciate risk as much as the next guy, but without the strength and endurance necessary to pull my share of the load, I wouldn't be doing anyone any favors by coming along. And even more important than getting a team of Black climbers to the summit of Denali was bringing everyone home safely.

Almost immediately upon returning from Mount Baker, I scheduled an appointment with an orthopedic specialist to explore the pain I had experienced. It turned out I had a series of arthritic bone spurs on both my left and right hips. The solution was a surgical procedure to replace the joints with prosthetic implants. My doctor assured me that I'd eventually be as good as new. I took the news of a double hip replacement with a surprising sense of optimism. I wasn't going to be on the summit team, but after two operations six weeks apart and another six weeks of rehabilitative therapy, I would be able to travel to Alaska, walk comfortably, and carry moderate loads in a backpack. I wasn't going to be a member of Expedition Denali, but I still had a role to play. I could still chronicle the landmark event.

From the start I had planned to write a book about this project. Even if I didn't summit with the group, as team journalist, it would still be my responsibility to share the expedition with the world. And though my personal journey would be limited to sending out dispatches of the team's progress from the NOLS office in Palmer, Alaska, our primary mission was still on track.

DELVING INTO THE PRELIMINARY RESEARCH FOR THIS BOOK, I DISCOVered a great deal about the role African-Americans have played in the outdoor realms of exploration, discovery, and adventure. Expedition Denali was simply the latest tale in a centuries-old narrative.

Despite a long history of slavery and racial discrimination, African-Americans have been directly involved in virtually all aspects of exploration from the very beginning. A Spanish navigator of African descent named Pedro Alonso Niño piloted the Santa Maria when Christopher Columbus first landed on North America's shores in 1492. Known as El Negro, he went on to explore much of the New World.

After the establishment of the United States, Black explorers were part of the exploration and western expansion of settlers across the plains, over the Rockies, and to the Pacific Ocean. From 1804 to 1806, an African-American slave named York was a full member of the Lewis and Clark Expedition. It is said that his presence as a person of color helped to forge relationships with the Native American communities they encountered along the way.

Throughout the Civil War and during emancipation, freed Black slaves actively participated in the settling of the West. In an ironic turn, Black troops who were instrumental in defeating the Confederate States of the South played a critical role in the displacement of Native Americans during the Indian Wars. But these men would earn the respect of the tribes they fought and became revered for their warrior spirit. And at the turn of the twentieth century, Black members of the US Cavalry, known as the Buffalo Soldiers, proved essential to the creation of the first national parks in Yellowstone, Yosemite, and Kings Canyon.

From the discovery of the North Pole in 1909 through the time of the Civil Rights Movement of the mid-1960s, African-American adventurers helped pave the way toward the modern era of technical mountaineering and Arctic exploration. Matthew Henson, the first person to stand on the North Pole, was a Black man from Baltimore, Maryland. And the first African-American to summit Denali, a Boeing engineer named Charlie Crenchaw from Seattle, Washington, did so in 1964—the same year the Civil Rights Amendment was signed into law.

Today, much of this history has been forgotten. And African-Americans comprise only a small percentage of people who routinely spend time in nature. Low rates of participation among people of color in adventure sports such as backpacking, rock climbing, downhill skiing, and mountaineering suggest troubling prospects for the future. Very few Blacks join environmental protection groups such as the Sierra Club or The Wilderness Society. And an even smaller number can be counted among the corps of professionals in careers dedicated to the preservation and conservation of nature, including national park rangers, foresters, or environmental scientists.

It's estimated that by 2042, the majority of US citizens will be nonwhite. Which begs the question: What happens when a majority of the population has neither an affinity for nor a relationship with the natural world? At the very least, it becomes less likely that future generations will advocate for legislation or federal funding to protect wild places, or seek out job prospects that aim to protect it.

The purpose of Expedition Denali—and by extension this book—is to demonstrate real-life examples of people of color who venture into the natural world for the sole purpose of adventure. Because everyone—regardless of their race, ethnicity, or socioeconomic status—should have the opportunity to experience and thrill in nature if they are so inclined.

The historic climb that took place in the summer of 2013 stands not as a grand gesture of personal achievement, but rather a sincere expression of welcome to those who dare follow. This team of Black American climbers made their ascent of Denali to extend an invitation, particularly to minority youth, to experience true freedom, to get outside and explore the divide between mediocrity and excellence. That boundary between the many who play it safe and the few who push beyond their limitations to achieve great things in the natural world is the adventure gap that people must cross to fulfill their dreams, no matter how foolish or frivolous.

CHAPTER ONE

An Expedition Begins

A MILITARY GREEN SCHOOL BUS ROLLED DOWN THE GRAVEL DRIVEWAY into a sprawling campus of neatly organized rustic buildings. Freshly mown lawns edged by mature trees created the orderly effect of an academic institution—and stood in direct contrast to an ancient barn with a corrugated tin roof, an expansive vegetable garden, two plastic hoop houses, and a pigpen. The NOLS students, instructors, and administrators who live here in Palmer, Alaska, lovingly call it the Farm.

As the nine members of Expedition Denali descended from the bus, they were filled with excitement, enthusiasm—and a touch of apprehension. An eclectic crew from diverse backgrounds, they arrived at the Farm prepared to each play their role as part of a team. This group was not your typical mountain-climbing team—which is so often white, privileged, and mostly male. Indeed, that was the point. Composed entirely of African-Americans, Expedition Denali had banded together to climb one of the world's highest peaks to shine a spotlight on the changing face of the sport and inspire a new and more diverse generation of climbers.

Their backgrounds were remarkably varied. Three—Tyrhee Moore, Erica Wynn, and Rosemary Saal—were college students. The others were Stephen DeBerry, an entrepreneur; Ryan Mitchell, a science teacher; Adina Scott, a mechanical engineer; Scott Briscoe, an outdoor educator; Stephen Shobe, an AT&T telephone tower technician; and last but hardly least, Billy Long, a bartender and part-time student from Brooklyn, New York. A deep love of climbing and a conviction that it should not be the sport of a lucky few had brought them together.

While the group had trained together a few times over the past eighteen months, they were still learning about one another. The training missions in the Chugach and on Mount Baker, as well as two other NOLS courses in the Patagonian Andes of Chile and the Waddington Range in British Columbia, had forged them into a team not just of climbers but of friends. Only Ryan, an undergraduate instructor of science at DeVry University in Philadelphia and a late addition to the expedition, was unfamiliar with the dynamics of the group that had already experienced so much together in the field. A quiet man of scholarly bearing, Ryan was at first slow to join in the jokes and good humor of the other participants. That would soon change as he settled into place as a full member of the team.

Everyone quietly surveyed the grounds and the mountains beyond, excited to finally be in Alaska. For some it was their second time at the Farm. The year before, Scott, DeBerry, and Billy had launched their two-week trip through the Chugach from here. And Tyrhee had spent the previous summer working in the outfitting bays. The others just took in their surroundings—they liked what they saw. Each of them had been thinking about this moment—and planning for it—for a long time now, and they were happy. After months of training, the time had finally come to test themselves on North America's highest peak.

The anticipation and nervous energy were almost palpable in the warm summer air.

As everyone milled around the bus, an athletic blond woman in a baseball cap appeared and greeted them warmly. The NOLS Alaska director, noticeably pregnant, was enthusiastic, as excited to see her new guests as they were to be there.

"Hey, everybody," she said cheerfully. "I'm Janeen Hutchins. Welcome to NOLS Alaska."

The nine newcomers came in closer. Hutchins rattled off a series of instructions that set the team in motion, issuing her orders with the kind but authoritative tone of a schoolmarm leading a class of wide-eyed children on a field trip. Each member of the team obediently hauled their personal gear from the roof racks and rear storage compartment of the bus to one of several open equipment bays. As they went about their work, the four course leaders, the Instructor Team or I-Team, emerged from one of the nearby buildings to survey their work. It was Saturday, June 8, 2013, and Expedition Denali had officially begun.

The lead instructor for the expedition was Aaron Divine, a Denali climbing veteran. Aaron put the group to work right away, unpacking and sorting their gear and personal items. Clothing, small electronic gadgets, and cooking utensils piled onto the concrete floor as people sifted through what they would either leave behind or carry with them for three weeks on the mountain.

The I-Team also included Madhu Chikkaraju, a talented climber and professional mountain guide from Bangalore, India. On the expedition as well was senior NOLS instructor James Kagambi, known as KG. This native of Kenya had logged more field days than any other instructor at NOLS, and in 1989 was the first Black African ever to reach the summit of Denali.

Clipboard in hand, the fourth I-Team member, Robby ReChord, reviewed every climber's equipment, checking each item against a master list as he cycled through the team members. It was his job to make sure that the climbers were equipped with the necessary gear for their trip. Having assembled his own gear kit from years of cast-off and secondhand items, Robby marveled to see the team's mostly new products, some still in plastic with the tags attached.

DeBerry's personal mountaineering inventory in particular featured the latest trends in color and style. Even the basics—long underwear, warm socks, gloves, knit cap, and sunglasses—had been assembled with an eye for fashion. As he pared down to the bare essentials, he emphasized keeping those items that were lightweight but warm and durable. By the end, DeBerry not only had everything he needed, he also looked sharp.

DeBerry is a former college athlete in track and field at UCLA and a Marshall Scholar with master's degrees in social anthropology and business administration from the University of Oxford. His mountaineering accomplishments include a summit of Kilimanjaro in 1997. Together with teammate Stephen Shobe, DeBerry is a member of the Pioneer Climbing Expedition, which aims to become the first team of African-Americans to climb the Seven Summits. Although it was difficult for him to leave his business behind and to be away from his family for so long, he simply couldn't turn down this opportunity to add Denali to his list.

In addition to the standard gear, the team members had each brought a puffy insulated parka with a hood, a synthetic fleece jacket, a waterproof breathable shell, insulated pants, waterproof snow pants, insulated overmittens, insulated booties, mountaineering boots, and gaiters. A man of modest means, Billy was thrilled with the assortment of technical clothing donated by The North Face. He folded each piece thoughtfully.

Together the system of layers would protect him from harsh wind and low temperatures as he ascended toward the summit. Though he was grateful for the gear's technical capabilities, he secretly couldn't help but imagine how sporty he'd look several months later walking the streets of New York City, a cool cat in a Gore-Tex jacket with legit mountain cred.

Billy might be described as a Renaissance man. Although he has no formal training in any organized sports, he is a natural-born athlete who enjoys most any pastime that allows him to challenge his strength and courage. Billy's interest in climbing was originally piqued by Jon Krakauer's *Into Thin Air*. Always one to live in the moment, his passion for travel and adventure has taken him from the bustling cities of China to the jungles of Central America. He has even been known to hop a plane to points unknown just to work on his foreign language skills for a few months at a time. He is a man of great introspection and an avid reader who aspires to be a writer. On Expedition Denali, he was seeking a pure adventure that he hoped to share with others someday.

Every item of technical clothing served a crucial role in an intricate and functional layering system to keep the wearer warm and dry but flexible. As they put on their new mountain gear, everyone felt a bit more confident in their abilities. They not only looked the part but *felt* like the climbers they were. But they also knew that all the fancy clothing in the world could never be more important than their months—and for some, years—of training and experience.

Because keeping weight to a minimum is crucial for mountaineering, everyone was encouraged to take along as little nonessential gear as possible. Reviewing the piles of goods, Robby cast aside extraneous items with respectful disdain, asking simply, "Do you really need this?"

But of course there were exceptions. As a fast-moving entrepreneur, DeBerry insisted on remaining in contact with his office and his family during the three weeks he would be on the mountain. He was given permission to bring along his satellite phone, even though such a thing is typically not allowed on a NOLS trip. Meanwhile, Rosemary had packed a white furry legless creature with black-yellow eyes that she called Ghosty. Nineteen-year-old Tyrhee clutched in his well-muscled arms a blue plush space alien with oversized ears. With none of the self-conscious bravado so common among teenaged boys, he smiled and stated simply, "Senzo goes everywhere with me."

A journalism student at the University of West Virginia, Tyrhee had already garnered an extensive climbing resume during two previous NOLS mountaineering courses. Tall and solidly built, Tyrhee is a handsome young man with a perpetual broad smile and warmth of spirit that's infectious. He had been introduced to the outdoors a few years earlier through the City Kids Wilderness Project in his hometown of Washington, DC, and had received a full tuition scholarship to fund his outdoor education. Now he hoped to begin a lifelong career working in the outdoors.

Tyrhee frequently visited his old neighborhood and connected with kids from his high school and middle school, where he had become something of a minor celebrity. He relished his role as someone who could provide an alternative view of the prospects and opportunities available to teenagers and young adults. The younger students looked up to him as someone with a similar background and experience who had not only gone on to better things, but seemed to be having a lot of fun. It's largely through role models like Tyrhee that NOLS demonstrates the various ways young people can enjoy a lifestyle that includes outdoor recreation.

FOUNDED BY PROFESSIONAL MOUNTAIN GUIDE PAUL PETZOLDT IN 1965, NOLS was established to provide specialized training for the best possible outcome in any wilderness experience. Petzoldt realized from his outdoor experiences with Outward Bound that wilderness training often lacked a strong code of ethical behavior that made protection of the environment a top priority.

With NOLS, Petzoldt hoped to educate and inspire a new breed of field instructors who would teach not only surviving in the wilderness but protecting it as well. In the process, he hoped to create a full-fledged conservation movement.

In many ways, Petzoldt has succeeded beyond his wildest dreams. NOLS has provided tens of thousands of men and women with the skills necessary to spend pleasant and productive time in nature while protecting the outdoors and natural resources. Clients come from a wide variety of professions, ranging from elementary school teachers to environmental scientists to astronauts working on the International Space Station. With campuses around the world, NOLS has had a profound influence that goes far beyond the geographical boundaries of language, nationality, and culture. Perhaps that's why NOLS administrators became concerned that, despite that progress, the majority of their students, faculty, and staff still consist of affluent, well-educated white people.

If this enrollment trend continues, especially as the US population begins to shift toward a nonwhite majority, that kind of mostly white enrollment could eventually make NOLS obsolete or even irrelevant. "What it means to be irrelevant is that we shrink and shrink until we cease to exist as a school," says NOLS manager of diversity and inclusion Aparna Rajagopol-Durbin.

Today NOLS aims to inspire a new generation of environmental stewards who better reflect the diverse landscape of America. The school is making a concerted effort to create a student body and staff that share Petzoldt's original vision of best practices in the wild. It is also working to educate a cadre of individuals who return home to their communities to educate and inspire others. Many conservation groups acknowledge the importance of diversity and profess a desire to make significant changes, but NOLS walks the talk, committing time and financial resources to building a community that is more diverse and inclusive of people of all races and ethnicities. They are doing this by reaching out to the segment of the population statistically least likely to spend time in nature: African-Americans.

AT THE FARM, EXPEDITION DENALI TEAM MEMBER ROSEMARY reviewed her kit with the meticulous care of an experienced mountaineer. A fair-skinned biracial woman with a sprinkling of freckles across her nose and a thick mop of brown curly hair, twenty-year-old Rosemary has a jubilant personality and a sharp and creative mind. Though still in college, she was already a graduate of the NOLS Waddington Range mountaineering course. Over the previous summer, she had spent nearly a month in the field practicing glacier travel techniques, crevasse rescue skills, and winter camping. Familiar with long days under the weight of a pack, Rosemary knew the value of minimizing the weight of her personal gear, but in addition to her stuffed companion, Ghosty, she had packed a large bag filled with hard candy, Oreo cookies, and mini-Clif bars. Though hardly out of high school herself, Rosemary has the inspiring personality and life skills necessary to help guide young people interested in following her example and becoming an accomplished outdoorswoman. Working with youth in the community where she was raised, Rosemary served as a member of the advisory board of YMCA's Passages Northwest, now called Girls Outdoor Leadership Development, in Seattle, where she empowered young women through the arts and outdoor education.

That first day at NOLS Alaska, Rosemary knelt on the concrete floor of the equipment bay surrounded by the enormous assortment of gear she planned to carry up the mountain. As she scanned the various items, she couldn't help but stop and think about how fortunate she was to have this opportunity. When she was younger, Rosemary lacked the resources to venture into the outdoors on her own or to buy her own equipment. But thanks to the organizations she has worked with, she was given many opportunities to experience nature throughout her formative years. She acquired the skills and expertise necessary to work and play comfortably in the field as a program participant and youth volunteer. She was now equipped to hold her own on one of the highest peaks in the world, and her greatest hope was to pay it forward by helping others to do the same.

Though they were considered the "kids" on the Expedition Denali team, Rosemary and Tyrhee came prepared with a wealth of knowledge and experience that rivaled that of the adults on the team. Alongside the stuffed animals they packed up with their ice axes and crampons, they possessed a maturity that enabled them to appreciate the purpose of this project and the vital role they played in it. Denali for them was more than just a mountain. It was a rite of passage.

Twenty-one-year-old Erica of Queens, New York, a beautiful young woman with the legs of a track star, was the expedition's third-youngest member. At the time of Expedition Denali, Erica was studying psychology and communications at American University. Though she had only recently discovered her interest in mountaineering, Erica aspired to be an example of healthy living through education and advocacy in her community. Introduced to the outdoors through GirlTrek, an organization dedicated to inspiring active lifestyles among Black American women of all ages, Erica first became an avid runner and then a cyclist. She eventually qualified for a scholarship for a NOLS Alaska backpacking course and later a thirty-day mountaineering course in Patagonia. Though Erica had no formal training in sports when she was growing up, she is naturally athletic and has an innate talent as a climber. Her proficiency at mastering backcountry skills opened up a whole new world. Recognizing the profound effect the outdoors had on her life, Erica realized that the time had come to change how women and people of color think and feel about spending time in nature.

Taking a break from the chores of packing, Erica wandered over to one of the many outbuildings on the Farm that served as office space and classrooms. She came upon an extensive library lined with books describing the flora and fauna of the Alaska Range, information on the geological formation of the mountains, and accounts of the many expeditions that had taken place not far from where she stood. As she perused the volumes before her, Erica was reminded that many of these stories were dominated almost exclusively by the adventures and exploits of white men.

Young people are exposed to many narratives, and Erica felt strongly that these stories shape our expectations of ourselves and of our lives. It's problematic if we're exposed to a single story and we can't identify ourselves in that story. Like so many young children, Erica had grown up in a culture heavily influenced by Disney movies and found herself unable to relate to the characters in those stories. *The white woman in those movies always gets the happy ending and she rides off with her Prince Charming*, she thought. *Where is my place? My happy ending?*

Erica thought of what little Black girls would make of the mountaineering stories like those in the library. They'd think they didn't have a place, or that the odds were stacked against them. She knew Expedition Denali could help change that. It could add a new story, and in that way, help women identify themselves in the outdoors in a way they were unable to in the past.

BY THE TIME THE TEAM HAD CAREFULLY REPACKED ALL THEIR GEAR, each of their backpacks stood at least three feet high. With sleeping bags, ice axes, helmets, crampons, carabiners, harnesses, prusiks, and avalanche beacons, individual gear came to more than forty pounds. But that did not include their shared equipment. Those items—ropes, tents, stoves, fuel, maps, shovels, crevasse probes, snow pickets, and parameter wands—still needed to be distributed evenly among them. Their meal rations—enough nutrition to sustain them all without resupply for almost a month of high-altitude climbing—were to be divvied up as well. By the time the outfitting was complete, each team member would be responsible for carrying as much as eighty pounds.

Once everyone's backpacks had been fully loaded, weighed, and inspected by the I-Team, Expedition Denali was ready for the mountain. The only gear that remained accessible was their tents and sleeping bags. The team would spend the night before their departure in the meadow on the western edge of the Farm campus. That evening, they took full advantage of all the modern amenities at their disposal: flush toilets, hot showers and spotty wireless Internet access, which they used to check their email and update Facebook.

Adina struggled desperately—but futilely—to get her laptop online. A pending job application had her on edge, and she was unable to confirm that all the necessary documents had gotten to her prospective employer. As a result, she was more worried about what the future would hold upon her return than the long climb ahead. Frustrated and anxious, she had trouble maintaining her usually sunny demeanor and eventually turned sullen.

An expedition requires complete dedication and focus, and one of the great challenges all mountaineers face is putting out of their minds all those things at home they can do nothing about. While DeBerry was sad about the time he would spend away from his wife and children, Billy mourned the loss of his music collection. Tyrhee already missed his mother, and Shobe was pissed off because, despite being over the age of fifty, he was technically a student on a NOLS course and, like younger members of the expedition, he couldn't join the I-Team at the staff house for a beer. "Damn it, I'm a grown man!" he grumbled.

At the root of everyone's anxiety on the eve of their departure was the knowledge of what lay ahead. The three-week journey would take its toll not just on their bodies but on their hearts and minds as well. Gradually, everyone quietly put aside their personal anxieties. Adina resigned herself to accepting that her job application had probably been received. DeBerry and Tyrhee each made one last call to their families to say good-bye. Billy tucked away his iPod. And Shobe rallied his own spirits and encouraged everyone to embrace the adventure that was about to unfold before them.

When the dinner bell rang, the team assembled on the covered deck off the kitchen, an outdoor pavilion known as the Bandstand. Dinners at NOLS Alaska primarily featured produce grown in the organic garden just a few hundred yards away. Hearty dishes and fresh bread were prepared daily by the cook staff.

Everyone took their place in the chow line, mingling freely with the NOLS staff and the members of other courses getting ready to depart on adventures of their own. Everyone chatted amicably, getting acquainted with other young people from across the country who shared a mutual passion for and interest in the outdoors.

That moment—as a racially diverse group of outdoor enthusiasts gathered to dine under the perpetual daylight of the Alaskan summer—illustrated the ultimate goal of the expedition. Though the team wouldn't leave for Denali until the next morning, that night on the Farm, enjoying conversation and heaping plates of delicious food, many of them felt that they had already arrived.

CHAPTER TWO

Diversity in the Mountains

THE STORY OF ONE YOUNG MAN WHO IS NOT PART OF EXPEDITION Denali, but could well be someday, shows the importance of bridging the adventure gap. Dwayne Smallwood, a nineteen-year-old student of environmental science at the Community College of Aurora in Colorado, spent the summer after his freshman year in 2011 helping to reestablish a colony of native plants to create a more diverse ecological landscape at Rocky Mountain National Park. Thanks in large part to Denver's Environmental Learning for Kids program—ELK for short—Smallwood had spent much of his youth discovering the wonders of nature and many summers working in service to public lands, so a job with the National Park Service was a natural fit.

"I've got scars from clearing brush and building trails at Rocky Mountain National Park," he told me with a smile and a hint of pride.

The son of a working mother and an estranged father, Smallwood grew up in a poor urban neighborhood, surrounded by steel and concrete, not mountains and trees. But thanks to ELK, he found a second home in nature. He hiked and went fishing, and he learned how to camp, cook outdoors, and sleep comfortably in a tent—all things most people who live close to the wilds of the Colorado Rockies take for granted. With the help of mentors like ELK cofounder Scott Gilmore, who were conscientious and caring, Smallwood acquired a profound appreciation and love of the wilderness. Now he wants nothing more than to work in a national park year-round.

"Scott basically brought me to the experience and said do whatever you want to do," Smallwood said. "I can be a scientist, a business person, whatever, he said, just be successful. This is success for me, going down this path."

Motivated by a strong desire to spend time in nature while working to protect it, he was determined to turn his childhood pastime into a worthwhile career. And judging from his enthusiasm for his work, he was well on his way toward the career in conservation that he wanted. "I want to work for the Colorado Division of Wildlife," he says "or hopefully for the National Park Service." Though that may not sound like such an unusual dream to some, it's not a particularly common aspiration for a young Black man.

Many would like to believe that race no longer matters when it comes to the career choices we make, where we live, where we play, or how we relate to the world around us. And for the most part, it doesn't. Thanks to the hard work, courage, and sacrifices of previous generations, the institutions that once prevented people of color from participating in any activity they desired no longer exist. Institutionalized slavery, of course, is long gone, as is legal segregation and housing and employment discrimination. The racially motivated violence rampant throughout the 1960s—cross burnings and Black Americans hung from trees—is a thing of the past. But what remains are cultural artifacts, social cues that define the unwritten sets of expectations we have for what people of a certain racial or ethnic background are supposed to do as part of "normal behavior." For many minorities in this country, these expectations do not include embracing the outdoors, whether for sport or for work. Despite advances in so many other aspects of our society, there is a racial divide between those who participate in outdoor activities and those who don't, a yawning chasm I call "the adventure gap."

That observation is supported by statistics. The modern outdoor enthusiast is typically white, well educated, financially secure, and socially mobile. A 2010 Outdoor Recreation Participation survey conducted by the Outdoor Foundation reported that of 137.8 million US citizens engaged in outdoor activities, 80 percent were Caucasian, a trend that is also reflected in the demographics of those who chose wilderness protection as a career. The National Park Service reported in 2010 that white men occupied 51 percent of positions at that agency and white women, 29 percent. These numbers are similar to those of other land and resource management agencies, such as the Bureau of Land Management and the US Forest Service.

These statistics become significant when compared against the demographic profile of the nation as whole. According to Dr. Nina Roberts, an assistant professor and social scientist from San Francisco State University, though African-Americans represent 12.6 percent of the US population, they typically make up a lower proportion of national park visitors (around 5–6 percent, depending on the region). Even with a sharp increase since 2006, "minorities still remain well below the number of visits of their white counterparts in proportion to their population across the United States," says Roberts.

The adventure gap is further reinforced by the national media and popular culture, which still tend to portray most mountaineers as relatively affluent, socially mobile Caucasians. Popular magazines, films, and commercial advertisements depict mountain climbers as square-jawed white men with blond hair and blue eyes. Obviously a reflection of the Northern European heritage from which contemporary mountain culture is derived, these images in media encourage the stereotype of what a mountaineer looks like. Americans across the racial spectrum view climbing and other outdoor activities as one of the "things white people do." Year after year, statistics reveal that African-Americans are least likely, of all ethnic groups, to engage in outdoor recreation, to be members of conservation groups or to pursue careers in wildlife management. Few African-Americans can be counted among professional athletes in the sports of rock climbing, mountain biking, kayaking, or downhill skiing. And in the multibillion-dollar outdoor industry, the number of Black senior executives can be counted on the fingers of one hand.

There is a link between recreating in the outdoors and wanting to protect it. People who spend time outdoors have the opportunity to appreciate its beauty and importance. Individuals across the nation and around the world who recognize the benefits of having access to fresh air, clean water, and open green space for their health and well-being will devote time and money to preserve those qualities. Having created loyal and long-standing relationships with the places they love most, they will pass their affection down to their children, establishing a legacy of stewardship that spans generations.

When people of color decide to climb, kayak, or ski, there is much more at stake than simply how people choose to spend their leisure time. The child who has never experienced the Grand Canyon, Devils Tower, Half Dome, the Painted Desert, or the Petrified Forest knows little about these places and can hardly be expected to feel invested in their preservation.

While there are, of course, many ways to spend time in nature, few require the commitment and dedication necessary to become even a proficient mountaineer. Climbing demands both physical and mental strength, as well as perseverance and sacrifice. Long expeditions far from home and family in some of the most hostile environments on Earth demand total commitment. Given the inherent and ever-present risk of injury or even death, climbing perhaps illustrates better than any other sport the passionate and intense relationship that can exist between human beings and the natural world. Pitting themselves against the elements, climbers test their limits and abilities to the utmost.

Passion alone isn't enough. Climbing also comes with a hefty price tag. Travel and gear are expensive—particularly mountaineering gear. The average consumer could easily spend $2,000 just to get set up with a traditional climbing rack, ice screws, ropes, ice axes, slings, crampons, rock shoes, and so on. Like the achievement gap that limits social mobility and access to higher education or better job prospects, the adventure gap is widened by limitations in financial resources. Even if you're not trying to outfit yourself as a technical climber, most forms of outdoor recreation involve some kind of gear, and that gear tends to be pricey. A simple outing to visit a park or take a hike typically requires gas and access fees. In fact an Outdoor Foundation survey reported that 61 percent of those who take part in outdoor recreation had personal incomes that exceed the national average of $41,000 per year.

In 2011 the National Bureau of Economic Research reported that African-Americans still lag behind in wages, bringing in about seventy-five cents for every dollar earned by whites. And though climbers typically lead a hand-to-mouth existence in pursuit of their sport, the "dirtbag" lifestyle likely has little appeal to emerging Black professionals who might be the first in their families to attend college. And without the much-aspired-to earning potential or social mobility made possible by professional team sports like football, basketball, or baseball, few African-Americans will be drawn to climbing as a career or even a pastime.

Historical reasons may also account for why some African-Americans don't take pleasure in outdoor experiences. After four hundred years of slavery and forced outdoor labor, African-Americans migrated en masse to major US cities after the Civil War and the end of slavery. Even more left the rural communities of the South during the Great Depression. Jim Crow laws and other forms of discrimination restricted movement and segregated minorities to urban enclaves until the Civil Rights Act of 1964. White supremacist groups typically perpetrated their acts of violence against minorities in wooded areas beyond city limits. Given this legacy, it's no wonder that African-Americans have often preferred to remain close to home.

Social scientist Roberts is a woman of mixed ancestry who once worked for the National Park Service. Her firsthand and research experience confirms that many variables contribute to this complex issue.

"Factors such as perceived discrimination, socialization, and upbringing, fear of personal safety, concern about not having the right outdoor gear or equipment, and lack of knowledge and awareness," Roberts says, "are a few of the many reasons African-Americans provided for lack of visitation to outdoor environments."

Though segregation is no longer legal and hate crimes are rare, the adventure gap is still there, a mysterious cultural barrier forged in social memory. While African-Americans collectively enjoy greater freedom, as individuals they may not feel free to adventure widely. Without the safety of numbers and locked doors, people of color may feel more vulnerable in the wilds of nature. They may opt to stay home, denying themselves and, potentially, future generations the opportunity to establish and enjoy a comfortable relationship with the outdoors.

The real question is: Why does it matter? Do we really need more people appreciating nature? US national parks receive 218 million visitors per year. Many of the most popular sites, such as Yellowstone and Yosemite, are typically filled to capacity; in some ways we are "loving our parks to death." Yet numbers aren't the main issue. What matters most is having a breadth and variety of individuals who are fully invested in supporting and protecting the parks into the future.

Many demographers project that the US population will consist of a majority of people of color by 2050 at the latest. According to William Frey, a research professor in population studies at the University of Michigan, and others, it will happen sooner than that.

"Because of the younger age structure (most minorities in the United States are under the age of twenty-five) and the somewhat higher fertility of new minorities in the United States, we may, by 2020, have a majority minority child population in the United States," Frey said in a radio interview. "And, of course, the Census Bureau has projected that by 2042, we'd have a majority minority total population—that is, less than 50 percent whites in the total population."

If outdoor enthusiasts are indeed mostly white, then a shift to a "majority minority" population in the United States could mean bad news for the conservation movement. As the ultimate responsibility to preserve and maintain public lands falls to state and federal governments, environmental protection groups must persuade a majority of voters to advocate for legislation and funding that supports environmental efforts. But if these groups' core constituency—affluent, well-educated white people—begins to shrink, so will their influence in the halls of Congress.

If this new demographic has little vested interest in environmental conservation, there will be fewer people to advocate for land and wildlife conservation and wilderness preservation.

Long term, therefore, the adventure gap and the problem of low minority involvement in outdoor activities could affect the preservation of the environment as a whole. The need for greater diversity in outdoor recreation is more than a matter of who's out enjoying the wilderness. Inclusivity will be a critical factor in the continuing viability and influence of the environmental movement.

As Dwayne Smallwood works to restore native plants for the National Park Service, he brings more to the experience than merely his manual labor. As a person of color, he is an ambassador, paving the way for others to follow his lead and play a more critical role in protecting the environment.

"We're making Rocky Mountain National Park look good!" he said as he pointed out his plant restoration project.

Smallwood was one of only two African-Americans on staff that season. But being one of very few people of color there makes little difference to him.

"It really doesn't matter," he says. "It was weird at first coming in because everyone else was second year. They'd all been here before. But they accepted me in and now they're teaching me things."

Though Smallwood is aware that he has a lot to learn, he has begun to carve out a place for himself in the profession of protecting public lands. He understands that his success at the National Park Service will depend not on his skin color but on his own dedication, hard work, and love of nature.

"Right now I'm just glad to wear the uniform," he says. "It makes me official, like I'm part of the park."

If we can agree that it is vital for the US population as a whole—regardless of race or ethnicity—to feel invested in the preservation of public land in general and the national parks in particular, then the question becomes: How do we actively engage and encourage young people like Smallwood to get involved?

Expedition Denali is one step. The project's goal is not to correct past wrongs of racial oppression or to take a stand in the face of discrimination, but instead to celebrate the gift of freedom that exists today in the outdoors and to affirm a positive role for people of color in outdoor recreation and environmental conservation. Defying the cultural traditions of the past, they want to show their community that they can mount and successfully complete an expedition to the top of America.

MY OWN TRAJECTORY THROUGH OUTDOOR RECREATION BEGAN AS IT has for many young men, through the Boy Scouts of America. Along with my friends and their dads, in 1975 my father Billy, my brother John, and I spent weekends tromping through the wilds of California's Griffith Park. I had the privilege of growing up with the children of other community leaders who were paving the way for a better life. My dad was one of the first African-Americans to graduate from UCLA law school. He raised me to aspire beyond the racial strife and discrimination that were so pervasive just a decade earlier and that still continued in many parts of the nation. That early exposure to the outdoors led me eventually to mountaineering.

As a teenager I remember how surprised I was to see the night sky when camped at 10,000 feet near the summit of Mount San Bernardino. As a kid in LA, I grew up surrounded by the bright lights of the city, which obscured all but a handful of stars. But there on that mountain, high above the clouds, the view was astonishing; the sky was crowded with so many twinkling lights it overwhelmed the senses. As I lay there in my sleeping bag under those stars, I felt as though I were just a tiny speck in an infinite universe, and also part of something grand and utterly beautiful.

After graduating with a four-year degree from the University of California, Berkeley, I took a job as a retail sales clerk at REI and also took up rock climbing. I spent my days selling hiking boots and sleeping bags, and my lunch hours climbing short routes at Indian Rock in the Berkeley Hills. On the weekends I drove to Yosemite Valley to play on the granite walls near the great El Capitan.

For twenty years now I've enjoyed a career in the outdoor industry, first as a salesman and now as a journalist. I've written hundreds of articles for magazines, newspapers, and online publications. When I first started in outdoor recreation, I was one of very few people of color working for a leading clothing and equipment manufacturer. Trading primarily on my enthusiasm for the lifestyle, I was welcomed and encouraged to excel in my chosen profession—and though I don't believe that being Black necessarily helped my career, I'm fairly certain it didn't hurt it.

Yet after two decades in the business, I see very few people of color entering the industry. Today, at national conventions, professional gatherings, and informal recreational events, I am usually the only Black person there. And I can't help but wonder how different the experience might be if there were more people in the profession who looked like me. Though I always find myself surrounded by friends and colleagues who share my passions and I never feel out of place, I also can't help but wonder, "Where are all the Black folks?"

As a journalist, I've tried to come to a better understanding of why this is still so and what factors apparently keep people of color from becoming involved in the activities I've come to love throughout most of my life. One day, something happened that made me realize exactly why finding the answer to this question was so important.

In January of 2009, I had the opportunity to interview Ken Burns, the documentary filmmaker, about his twelve-hour TV miniseries *The National Parks: America's Best Idea.* When I asked him how he planned to reach people of color with his film, he explained that his depiction of national park history included several stories about the many contributions that African-Americans, Asian-Americans, and Hispanics have made to the preservation of the wilderness. Nonprofit funding designed to encourage appreciation and a feeling of ownership of the national parks among minority groups across the country allowed Burns's team to go into the inner cities to say, in his words, "Let me tell you about Captain Charles Young of the Buffalo Soldiers, the first stewards and custodians of the national parks." Burns said, "Before there was a park service, there was no money to take care of them and the cavalry was essentially maintaining order in many parks, particularly in California. In Yosemite and General Grant Park then, it was the African-American Buffalo Soldiers. It's a wonderful heroic story."

In that moment my mind reeled at the revelation that a group of African-Americans had played a role in the preservation of national parks in the West and, in effect, in the creation of the National Park Service itself!

Many African-American youngsters learn about the Buffalo Soldiers, Black men assigned to the Twenty-Fourth Infantry and the Ninth and Tenth Cavalries of the US Army who rode the western range on horseback at the end of the nineteenth century. At the end of the Civil War, thousands of Black soldiers still wore the blue Yankee uniforms. Rather than return to the southern states to become farmers or migrate to the industrial North to work in factories, a large number of these newly emancipated citizens continued their national service, reenlisting in the army as career soldiers. Many of them headed west.

In the years that followed, these Black warriors distinguished themselves in the Indian Wars. Driven by a steadfast belief in Manifest Destiny, the US Army cut a bloody path from the east across the plains to the west, either systematically relocating or simply eradicating the Native American population to make way for white settlers to build their homes on captured territory. The Native tribes who encountered these ferocious and courageous men with black faces and wooly hair were reminded of one of their most sacred symbols—the buffalo—and, thus, called them Buffalo Soldiers.

LIKE OTHER CHILDREN, I'D GROWN UP HEARING STORIES ABOUT THE Buffalo Soldiers. But after more than two decades as a professional in the outdoor industry and a lifetime of visits to California's national parks, this was the very first time I had ever heard that the Buffalo Soldiers had spent any time there. I knew about Teddy Roosevelt's historic meeting with John Muir at Glacier Point in 1903. That was the stuff of legend and a pivotal moment in the enduring history of Yosemite. But little did I realize that in the same year, more than four hundred African-American cavalry men had made the three-week journey on horseback from the Presidio in San Francisco to Yosemite to patrol the park and keep it safe. From the earliest days of Yosemite, these Black men performed many of the same duties that national park rangers do today.

Burns's documentary also introduced me to someone who would deeply affect the way I viewed my own legacy. Shelton Johnson has been for many years the only Black ranger permanently stationed at Yosemite National Park. Today, he is also an accomplished writer and storyteller who pursued graduate studies in poetry before joining the National Park Service in 1981. As an interpretive ranger, Johnson has dedicated much of his career to sharing the Buffalo Soldiers' story.

Johnson has a melodic voice and impeccable articulation, and he shares his passion for the outdoors in words that are nothing less than poetry. In a scene from the Burns documentary, Johnson describes an unforgettable day from his own experience in Yellowstone National Park.

"One of the last jobs I had at Yellowstone was delivering the mail on snowmobile," he began. "There I was, in the world's first national park, and I remember going down into Haden Valley. There were bison crossing over the road, two-thousand-pound mammals crossing over the road. It was so cold; it was about sixty degrees below zero. And the bison, as they breathed, the air around them seemed to crystallize. And there were these sheets; these ropey strands of crystals kind of came flowing down from their breath. I saw them. They turned their heads and looked at me, and I remember thinking that had I not been on that machine I would have thought that I had been thrust fully back into the Pleistocene, back into the ice age."

I imagined what it would have been like at the turn of the century for the Buffalo Soldiers who might have come upon a similar scene of bison roaming over the land. Just as Johnson envisioned himself flung back into the prehistoric past, I pictured myself as an army private in 1903, wrapped in blankets and traveling through the snow on horseback in the middle of the Montana wilderness, perhaps to deliver the mail to a remote outpost. After years of war they must have thought that being awarded a duty station in the middle of the world's first national park was a dream. I felt for the first time a visceral connection to the past, a link between my own passion for the outdoors and the ancestral legacy of these Black American men who protected the parks so long ago.

Listening to Johnson, what struck me most profoundly was the realization that something had been missing from my life. The many years that I'd spent in nature suddenly took on new meaning as I discovered that men who looked like me—Black men with whom I share an ancient blood relationship as well as the tainted history of slavery and racial oppression—were part of the great history of the national parks I love. I found myself a bit overwhelmed with emotion because—for the first time—I felt like I truly belonged. No longer was I just an individual who'd gotten hooked on climbing and the joy of the outdoors. I realized that I was part of a long legacy of people of color who had immersed themselves in the outdoors—a legacy that dates back to the parks' very first days.

"I felt like this was the first day, and this morning was the first time the sun had ever come up. And the shadows that are being cast right now is the first time that shadows have ever been cast on the Earth," Johnson said as he continued to describe the bison. "I was all alone, but I felt I was in the presence of everything around me and I was never alone. It was one of those moments when you get pulled outside of yourself into the environment around you. I felt like I was with the breath of the bison. As they were exhaling and I was exhaling and they were inhaling, it was all kind of flowing together. And I forgot completely about the mail! All I was thinking was that a single moment in a place as wild as Yellowstone, or most of the national parks, can last forever."

Burns sent me a copy of his documentary and I played that scene over and over again. As I continued to ponder and visualize the Buffalo Soldiers in Yosemite and Yellowstone, it became something of an obsession. What I came back to again and again was this: How was it possible that I had never heard this story? And if I hadn't heard it, how many others hadn't heard it either? My interest in the issue of diversity in outdoor recreation had finally snapped into focus. It became clear to me that the best way to understand how we got to where we are today is to first know where we came from. And to do that, I had to start at the very beginning.

FASCINATED BY THIS BLIND SPOT IN MY UNDERSTANDING OF THE PAST, I headed back to Yosemite for a history lesson. In late July of 2009, several months before the release of the national parks documentary, I received an invitation to a series of press events to promote the forthcoming series. Over a long weekend I had the privilege of being one of a handful of reporters who followed Ken Burns around Yosemite on a scenic tour. Among the guests was none other than ranger Shelton Johnson.

During that visit, we had the good fortune to see Johnson in action. In a weekly summer presentation he gives to visitors at the Yosemite Theater, Johnson adopts the persona of a US Cavalry sergeant in a one-man stage show called *The Forgotten Yosemite: A Buffalo Soldier Remembers*. His performance brings to life the likely thoughts and impressions of a Black man serving in a remote wilderness duty station at the turn of the twentieth century.

Dressed in a period uniform, Johnson took his place in front of the audience. He stepped onto the brightly lit stage playing a haunting melody on a wooden flute. The song and the instrument he played are reminiscent of his own Native American heritage, as well as that of the many aboriginal tribes that once populated the woods and mountains of Yosemite Valley. Wearing a classic Stetson hat bearing the crossed saber insignia of the regiment in which his character served, Johnson stood erect, swaying slightly to the gentle rhythm of the music. He also wore a blue woolen coat with shiny brass buttons; the bright yellow stripes on his sleeves signified his rank as a noncommissioned officer.

Johnson concluded his song with a long note, allowing the sound to fade into silence. His spell cast, he finally spoke, "That's how I like to say hello."

In the folksy vernacular of the period, Johnson welcomed his guests, engaging the audience in the cheerful and cordial manner of a proud host. "How did you enjoy your walk through the park?" he asked with a broad smile. "Are these tall trees and high mountains, these sheer granite cliffs not magnificent! My name is Sergeant Elizy Bowman. Welcome, and I hope you enjoy your stay. I reckon you likely felt much the same way I did, the first time I came riding through the Central Valley with my company, Troop K, as we took up our duty station here in Yosemite. And I have to tell you, after years of fighting Cheyenne across the plains, the Spaniards in Cuba, and that long occupation of the Philippines, to be here under blue skies breathing this clean, clear air is nothing short of paradise."

Johnson goes on to tell the story of another Buffalo Soldier, Charles Young, who was also the first Black administrator of a national park. Racially motivated legislation was enacted beginning in 1876, the culmination of a decade of steady erosion of the liberties so hard fought for and won in the Civil War. So-called Jim Crow laws limited the freedom of Black Americans in the southern states of the former Confederacy and reinforced a nationwide perception of inferiority. These laws mandated segregation of most public facilities, including schools, restaurants, restrooms, and even drinking fountains, resulting in broad patterns of discrimination that made social advancement for people of color all but impossible. Though not codified through legislation in the northern or western states, the "separate but equal" doctrine was nevertheless pervasive, dividing the races through segregated housing, biased lending practices at banks, and prejudiced hiring preferences in the workplace. One of the few institutions where African-American men could distinguish themselves and rise to prominence was the US Army. In their capacity as representatives of the federal government, they carried weapons and enforced the law of the land with unprecedented authority.

Although Black American soldiers served in segregated regiments, they were nonetheless given the opportunity and resources to rise through the ranks. Holding themselves to a much higher standard than the white officers expected of them, Black enlisted men and noncommissioned officers were determined to prove that they were equal to their white counterparts in hard work, courage, and patriotism. Routinely given the toughest assignments—combat missions with little chance of survival or degrading, often humiliating, tasks—they went well beyond even the most ambitious expectations. The Army made it possible for aspiring Black men of exceptional talent to assume positions of leadership. One man who did so was Charles Young.

The third African-American to graduate from the military academy at West Point, Charles Young was the son of a former slave. His father had earned his freedom through service in the US Army as a soldier during the Civil War. Young was a diligent and tenacious scholar, graduating from an otherwise all-white high school near the top of his class to earn himself entry to the prestigious military training college. Though Young suffered no end of torment at the hands of white upperclassmen who did everything possible to drive him out, he persisted and endured. Fortunately, he enjoyed the camaraderie of a fellow Black cadet, John Hanks Alexander, who would become the first African-American in the US Armed Forces to hold a regular command position and the second Black graduate of West Point.

Commissioned as a second lieutenant upon graduation, Young was assigned to the Tenth US Cavalry Regiment at Fort Robertson in

Nebraska, the unit known by then as the Buffalo Soldiers. He later worked as a professor in the military sciences department at Wilberforce College in Ohio and then as an Army major during the Spanish-American War. In 1901 he was promoted to the rank of captain in the Ninth Cavalry Regiment.

In 1903, Young was appointed acting superintendent of Sequoia and General Grant national parks, the national parks being under the direct supervision of the US military at the time. That spring he led a regiment of five hundred Buffalo Soldiers on horseback from their base in the Presidio of San Francisco to set up operations in the parks. The first Black administrator of a national park, Young proved to be quite effective in achieving the long-term goals of his assignment, despite limited funding and a short building season between the long winters of the high Sierra Nevada.

It's estimated that Young and his men completed more work projects over the next several months than the previous military administration had in three years. The Buffalo Soldiers finished construction on the wagon road to the Giant Forest, where some of the world's tallest trees have grown for millennia. They established the road to the base of Moro Rock, a popular tourist destination with an exquisite western view of Sequoia National Park. They built the trail leading to the summit of Mount Whitney, the tallest peak in the lower 48 states. And by August of that year, park visitors had clear access by wagon to what had been some of the most remote areas in the region. Many of the roads and trails they worked on are still in use today.

In addition to the hard work of road building, the Buffalo Soldiers patrolled the parks for poachers, fought wildfires, thwarted illegal loggers, and generally kept the peace as law enforcement officers. Although many white visitors to the parks resented taking orders from Black men, the Buffalo Soldiers performed their duties with measured diplomacy, creating a solid sense of law and order in the wilderness. They served their country in an exemplary manner, despite the racial turmoil of the era. It's hardly a stretch to suggest that these early park rangers helped to set the standard of excellence for the institution that would in 1916 become the National Park Service.

"I always say that what separates any Buffalo Soldier from a white soldier is that the Buffalo Soldiers were always fighting on two fronts," Johnson told me after his performance. "There was the enemy before them, and that enemy called racism that completely surrounded them every day of their lives. In spite of that fact, they did their duty even though they carried a far heavier burden. They worked harder than their counterparts. They had to, just to prove that they could do the work at all."

Captain Young and his men made a lasting contribution to the preservation and even expansion of our nation's parks: Upon Young's recommendation, the secretary of the interior, Ethan A. Hitchcock, sought acquisition of private land surrounding Sequoia and expanded the park boundaries. Such facts of history make it all the more surprising that so few African-Americans visit the national parks today.

"It's doubly ironic to think that one hundred years ago there were more Africans or people of African descent in an official capacity in both Yosemite National Park and Sequoia National Park than there are today," Johnson said. "Think about how much the world has changed. The Buffalo Soldiers were here before there was a Malcolm X, before there was a Martin Luther King, before Shirley Chisholm, before all of these people that we know so well. They were here before the Civil Rights Movement. They were here at a time when race relations were at their most abysmal."

"So when I see myself wearing this uniform," he continued, "I'm also making a challenge that people of my culture can be a part of this history too, and know we are part of this history. And that is the value of the Buffalo Soldier story. It is stating that at the very beginning of this great invention and this great contribution to world culture, which is America's best idea, that we were part of it."

Just a few years later, on March 25, 2013, President Barack Obama designated the home of Charles Young in Xenia, Ohio, as a national monument to honor his great work as well as that of the other men who served as Buffalo Soldiers.

"The National Park Service shall coordinate with the Golden Gate National Recreation Area, which manages the Presidio in San Francisco, and Sequoia, Kings Canyon, and Yosemite national parks to commemorate the historical ties between Colonel Charles Young and his military assignments at those sites, and the role of the Buffalo Soldiers as pioneering stewards of our national parks," Obama proclaimed.

CHAPTER THREE

Hurry Up and Wait

THE MORNING FOLLOWING THEIR ARRIVAL IN ALASKA, EXPEDITION Denali's departure was somewhat delayed. The cooks in the kitchen, the gardeners tending their vegetables, the staff members at their computers all stopped work spontaneously to stream out and give the team hugs, take photos, and say good-bye. Their presence was a collective display of solidarity and support for the mission about to get under way. In any given season, more than a thousand students board buses bound for great adventures of all kinds—and normally they don't elicit such a reaction from the staff. But there was something special about this team and everyone knew it. They understood that these men and women were climbing not just for themselves but as an inspiration to others—particularly young people who might find themselves at the Farm for an adventure of their own someday.

I watched as Stephen Shobe rallied the team onto the bus. At fifty-six, Shobe was the oldest member of the Expedition Denali team. He was also the most experienced, and most of the climbers had begun to take their cues from him. Shobe had already ascended four of the Seven Summits, and he was eager to add the highest peak in North America to his accomplishments. Denali was the next notch in his belt in a long career spent in pursuit of ambitious goals.

Gregarious and confident, Shobe could always be counted on for a joke. With a gleam in his eye and a devilish grin full of flashing white teeth, he laughs easily and often, beginning with a chortling rumble from deep within his belly and erupting in big shrugs of his narrow but powerful shoulders. Tall and handsome, he is a striking figure with platinum hair and a mustache that stands in glaring contrast to his ebony skin. Though he has a day job stringing telephone wires and tending cell towers for AT&T, he is also a card-carrying member of the Screen Actors Guild of America and splits his leisure time between climbing and the occasional modeling job or TV commercial.

Shobe is also a natural leader and role model with a calm sense of discipline, which he brought to every aspect of climbing. Though he was not technically in charge, during training he had made a habit of putting himself out in front. While Shobe never presumed to be the boss, his confidence inspired those around him to back his every play.

Even after many years as a climber, Shobe approached each new adventure into the wild with the excitement and enthusiasm of a rank beginner. As we sat talking about the upcoming expedition, the balls of his feet bounced on the floor with barely contained energy, as though he were planning to spring into action at any moment.

I was curious about his past and the source of his joyful spirit. He grinned and his eyes twinkled as he launched into his story. Shobe was four when his family moved into a brand new house in an unincorporated part of Los Angeles County near what is now Compton, California. In 1960, this was one of the first areas where Black Americans could purchase and own a home outside of southcentral Los Angeles. Although infamous today for its rampant street crime—commonly referenced in gangster rap lyrics—Compton then was on the bucolic margins of the suburban frontier.

Shobe and his brothers experienced the region's final days as an agrarian landscape, a time when LA County still had dairy cows. On the edge of the enclave was an open field, owned by a local farmer, where they often played. To their young eyes, it seemed limitless.

Whenever rain fell, the vacant properties near his home filled with water and transformed into a ready-made lake. Shobe and his brothers played Huck Finn and Tom Sawyer and imagined themselves navigating the shores of the Mississippi River through Mark Twain's Missouri. Though this make-believe Hannibal was likely no bigger than fifty by twenty feet across, to them it was vast.

Shobe recalls his youth as a time when children were more creative, when play was an unpredictable exploration of railroad tracks that extended to a destination discoverable if only they could walk far enough before night fell and they were called home to dinner. They dared one another to peek down the long tunnels of sewer drains. Though there was light at the end, who among them was brave enough to shimmy through the narrow pipe on elbows and knees to reach the other side? Even as an adult, Shobe shivered at the memory of his terror at the prospect, and yet I detected a tiny gleam of regret in his eye for not having tried. It appeared that Shobe had always had his sights set on the unknown.

In high school Shobe participated in typical urban sports. He was on the verge of distinguishing himself as a pole-vaulter, but a broken leg turned him off competition. Fearful of breaking something else, he quit the sport and turned his attention to other interests.

When it came time to apply to college, he approached the office of his senator for a recommendation to the Naval Academy at Annapolis.

Unfortunately, his application was denied. Hoping to plead his case for admission, he went to the senator's field office. He recalled that an aide said to him, "'I applaud your efforts and the grades that you have here, but because the high school that you're going to is substandard, I'm afraid that you will not be able to compete against the other applicants.' It was like it was a whites-only club, and the only way that you could get into it was to go to a white institution that was rated higher than Compton High."

Disappointed but not deterred, Shobe joined the US Navy as a common seaman. He served for three years on active duty and thirteen years in the Naval Reserves. There he honed his skills as a diver, received his flight training as a helicopter pilot, and eventually earned a spot on the staff of an admiral. Because of his outgoing personality and the strength of his character, Shobe managed to avoid much of the racial tension between service members and officers that was common in the military at the time. He quickly gained a reputation for, as he says, "not putting up with a lot of crap." The Navy, he found, extended a certain amount of privilege to white sailors in its ranks that was not always extended to Black sailors. Still, Shobe was well liked, respected, and admired by those around him.

Back in civilian life, Shobe returned to Los Angeles, got married, and took a job working for AT&T as a line technician. He started climbing in his spare time after his wife introduced him to the sport at Mount Rubidoux, a local bouldering area near Riverside, California.

Shobe was immediately attracted to the sport and its combination of athleticism and technical equipment. But from the first time he observed climbers ascending their routes, he thought they made it look much harder than it needed to be. Even while watching them that first time, Shobe felt he could do better. For Christmas that year his wife gave him a gift of his first rock climbing class and that was it. He was hooked.

Although Shobe started climbing only casually at first, he rapidly improved. He soon found himself spending many weekends in spots around Tuolumne Meadows and occasionally in Yosemite Valley. Shobe was often the only African-American on the mountain, but whether because of his gregarious nature or his genuine talent, he was quickly accepted by the other climbers in the small community as one of their own.

Shobe recalls being part of a photo shoot and film session with several other climbing friends to model a new line of apparel.

"It was at Dana Point near the sea cliffs," he said. "I was there climbing with everyone else, and I felt like I was as much a part of the project as anyone. But when it came time to see the clip, there was none of me in it. I suppose it was at that point I started to realize that there were no people who look like me in *Rock & Ice* or *Climbing* or *Alpinist* magazines. It made me wonder. Where are all the Black folks?" Shobe then couldn't help but notice that the companies whose gear he relied on—Metolius, Gramicci, Prana, and The North Face—never featured any people of color in any of their ads.

Shobe was struck by the fact that an entire segment of the population was being left out of his climbing experience. Judging from the media, Black folks didn't climb at all. But Shobe freely admitted that he was a minority within a minority.

As he explained to me, so many young people of color have no exposure to sports like climbing. Without role models and without access, "Many of them didn't know what these things were, and if they did know, they'd say, 'That's something white people do.'" Shobe wanted to change that. By ascending high mountains and living an exemplary life as an adventurer, he wanted to become that positive role model for young people in his community and demonstrate that people of color can and do aspire to accomplish many different things, including climbing mountains. And when it came to sports, he wanted the kids in his community to know that there are alternatives to football, basketball, and baseball. There are other ways for them to rise out of the circumstances of their urban life to achieve great things.

Several years ago Shobe set out on a quest to climb the Seven Summits and then bring his stories of adventure back to the inner city neighborhood where he grew up. He created his own nonprofit called the Pioneer Climbing Kids Foundation, establishing a platform from which he could share his message. And as a member of Expedition Denali, he was taking advantage of an excellent opportunity to talk to kids about adventure and impress upon them a simple idea: "If you can dream it, you can do it."

As he takes his stories of climbing the highest peaks in the world to schoolkids of all ages, Shobe opens windows of opportunity in the minds of young people of color.

"I once had a kid come up to me after a talk, and he says to me, 'Next time you go, can I come too?' Man, this child was four years old," he said. "When I can make a connection like that, that's when the magic happens."

THE EXPEDITION DENALI SCHOOL BUS FINALLY PULLED AWAY FROM the Farm around 11:00 A.M., bound for the town of Talkeetna, 81 miles away. The expedition would follow the West Buttress along a route originally pioneered by the great alpine explorer and photographer Bradford Washburn in 1951. From Talkeetna, the team would be ferried in small groups by turbo-prop cargo planes called Otters over to the south side of the mountain.

It was a beautiful cloudless day, and the sun had begun to beat down mercilessly. It was the warmest summer anyone in Alaska could remember, with uncomfortably high temperatures throughout the long days of enduring sunshine. A nerve-racking onslaught of swarming mosquitoes relentlessly bit every exposed piece of human flesh. But with the relative cool of the mountain to look forward to, the climbers didn't seem to mind. At the park service headquarters in Talkeetna, they sat and ate sack lunches they had prepared back at the Farm; they waited, mostly calm and relaxed with the sleeves of their long underwear tops rolled up to their biceps and their Gore-Tex jackets tied around their waists.

Before heading to the air base, everyone on their way to Denali receives a briefing from the climbing ranger at Denali National Park headquarters. Along with a lecture on the proper management of their human waste, the team received the good news that cooperative weather had made possible a record number of successful summit bids that season. More than 70 percent of those who had tried in recent weeks had made it to the top. Because of extreme cold and dangerously high winds, the success rate on Denali is typically closer to 50 percent.

But before the team could become overly optimistic, the ranger also let them know that the unseasonably warm temperatures in the higher elevations had also increased the risk of rockfall due to melting ice. Although the weather would offer milder conditions for climbing, routes that were generally made stable by freezing temperatures had become more dangerous and unpredictable. The possibility of avalanches grew more likely with each warm day that passed.

Warned of the hazards, the team reboarded the bus. Eager for the adventure ahead, they set aside any thoughts of impending doom during the ride to the edge of town and the landing strip at Talkeetna Air Taxi. The team would fly straight into base camp on the Kahiltna Glacier at

7,200 feet on the south side of Denali, thereby saving themselves more than a week of walking.

The team would haul every piece of equipment in backpacks and on sleds pulled behind each rope team of three. In order to efficiently move their supplies higher and higher up the mountain, rations of food and stove fuel were divided into portions that could be dropped off and retrieved between each successive campsite in a time-honored method of gradual ascent. Camps on the route across the Kahiltna Glacier would be established at 7,800 feet, 9,500 feet, 11,000 feet, 14,200 feet, and 17,000 feet. With the exception of the first long haul from the airstrip to Camp II, every move from one camp to the next would include a double carry.

After establishing each successive camp on the way up the mountain, the climbers would shed heavier items for sleeping and cooking—tents, sleeping bags, stoves, and fuel. Then with lighter packs, they would transport only the supplies needed for later in the trip to a spot about halfway between their current campsite and the next one. A double carry means having to traverse the same part of the route twice. But with significantly less weight to carry, that distance, though doubled, requires much less effort.

The cache of supplies would remain buried under a pile of snow marked with an identifying flag; when needed, the location might also be recorded as GPS coordinates. The cache could then be collected with light backpacks when the next camp was established the following day. With so much food and equipment to carry—leapfrogging forward from camp to cache to camp and back again—the process of climbing Denali would not only be physically demanding but time consuming as well. The entire route, from start to finish through each of the high-elevation campsites, would take at least fourteen days, though they planned to be on the mountain for three weeks or longer.

As soon as the bus pulled to a stop on the tarmac at the Talkeetna Air Taxi landing strip, everyone spilled out to unload their packs and other equipment from the roof of the bus and stow them in the three tiny planes that awaited them. When the aircraft finally set off on the short flight through the jagged mountains of the Alaska Range, team member Scott Briscoe sat on the edge of his seat, peering out the window. As the plane soared up into the sky and flew straight toward the snowcapped peaks, his heart rate rose steadily and his face broke into a wide grin.

"It changed from distant thoughts read in pages and images seen on the computer screen to a reality I was moving through and breathing in," he told me later. "I literally started laughing to myself in the plane out of pure excitement that it was actually happening."

Scott is a lifelong outdoor enthusiast with vast experience hiking and climbing in the northern Cascades, central Rockies, and southern Sierra Nevada. Back home in San Francisco, Scott works with low-income schools and young people with minimal exposure to the outdoors. At the time, he helped kids forge a lasting relationship with nature while managing nonprofit grant applications for the Bay Area office of the outdoor clothing company Patagonia.

Inspired by his grandfather, who loved to fish, Scott developed an appreciation for the natural world early on. With one parent Black, the other white, Scott is biracial. Scott has rugged features, a shaved head, and a gentle smile. Though he attended private schools and was granted many opportunities to experience high-intensity sports like skiing and snowboarding, Scott was no child of privilege; his opportunities came from the support and sacrifice of a single mom who encouraged his recreational passions. Eventually he built a career dedicated to giving others similar opportunities.

As the planes cruised through the valley, the peaks of Mounts Foraker, Hunter, and Hayes became visible in the distance, but an inversion layer of clouds made it impossible to see the peak of Denali. Even as the planes came upon it—the base of the mountain growing larger and larger with each passing moment—all that could be seen was the rising slope as it disappeared into a white void.

The planes skidded to a halt on the icy runway, and team members hustled to unload their gear and haul it to a central rallying point a few hundred yards from the airstrip. A previous expedition had abandoned a nearby campsite, which was sheltered from the wind behind a protective wall of ice. The group immediately set to work arranging their new quarters into a comfortable home on the glacier. They set up their tents, sorted out and stored their sharp items—ice axes and crampons—and set to work melting ice for water.

The sun beat down and the air was surprisingly warm. Although surrounded by ice and snow, the team stripped down to minimal layers, with just enough insulation to protect them from an errant gust of wind. They worked steadily through the evening, the daylight persisting well after the sun had set in the Lower 48.

As the Expedition Denali team leader, Aaron Divine was responsible for directing and overseeing the establishment of this first camp on the glacier. Lean and muscled, Aaron projected strength and authority. Not one to bark orders, Aaron expected to have his instructions followed without discussion. He was decisive, direct, and an economical manager of energy—his own as well as that of his team. He'd let people learn from their mistakes yet never say afterward, "I told you so."

The plan was for the team to make their first move early the next morning, within twelve hours of the last flight landing on the glacier—standard operating procedure for an experienced group of climbers.

Most guided trips spent an entire day at base camp going over different technical skills like knot tying and assembling a rope team, but Aaron had every confidence that this group already knew the fundamentals.

Ryan Mitchell, who had made an attempt of Denali the year before, settled comfortably into the chores of making camp. He first helped the others fortify the wind walls around their tents and then set about the task of preparing dinner with his cooking group. The hours grew later, but without the circadian cue of evening falling into darkness everyone was still energized and wide-awake.

Erica Wynn fumbled with the bite valve on her hydration pack. While she was climbing in Patagonia a year earlier, the device had frozen shut, and she busily worked to find a solution that would prevent that from happening again. Her prior experience had taught her many things about living and working in the high-altitude environment of a climbing expedition. But every mountain is different, and she had never climbed anything like Denali. She occupied her mind with finding a solution to a problem she had faced before and that was now within her immediate control. Once she had come up with a fix, she, like the others, settled down to sleep in anticipation of their first full day on Denali.

Unfortunately, the weather put an end to Aaron's ambitious plan for an early start the next day, day three after the expedition's arrival in Alaska. Morning arrived with a layer of clouds at ground level that had reduced visibility to only a few hundred feet; it would have been unwise to traverse the glacier in those conditions. Though it limited visibility and made traveling as a large group difficult, the fog itself wasn't the critical issue but rather an indication of something worse: the overnight temperature had never dropped below freezing to cement the ice bridges across the crevasses that were invisible throughout the path that lay before them. One of the biggest dangers on the Kahiltna is falling into a crevasse. During the heat of the day, rising temperatures soften and weaken the ice bridges that form over deep fissures in the glacier. As temperatures drop at night, those bridges become much more stable and are safer to cross. The team was eager to get started, but they decided to hold off for a bit. If the fog cleared, that meant the temperature had dropped sufficiently to make the ice bridges firm—and therefore safe—for travel.

But the weather continued to be uncooperative. As the sun warmed the glacier and further weakened the snow bridges with each passing hour, the probability of dangerously soft conditions increased. Throughout the trip, the most favorable time to travel would be during the late evening or early morning hours when conditions were coldest and the snow and ice was most solid and least likely to crack under the full weight of a climber with an eighty-pound backpack.

The possibility of a crevasse fall now seemed just as great as the risk of being caught in an avalanche. A technical ascent of most mountains involves more than the hazards of high altitude and falling. Timing is everything. In central Alaska, where the sun shines almost around the clock in summer, the windows of opportunity are not only few and far between, but they also have a tendency to unexpectedly shrink. The team finally gave up on the prospect of departing that day. Hanging around base camp, they had the opportunity to connect with a group of National Park Service rangers who were patrolling the mountain on a course of ascent parallel to theirs. The rangers were able to provide detailed information on the size and location of the many other groups heading up the West Buttress route. With nineteen climbers, including a media team—four cameramen and two additional guides—to record their progress, Expedition Denali was the largest team on the mountain. Knowing where the other parties were during the long journey would help the expedition to pace the location of their different camps on the way up.

To pass the time, the course instructors went over a variety of different training exercises to hone the climbers' skills. They practiced techniques ranging from self-arrest with an ice ax to crevasse rescue. Over the next several hours, team members carefully arranged their gear, distributing items into the plastic sleds each rope team would pull behind them. Though they were all eager to get started, no one was looking forward to that first long haul. "I knew what was coming next," Shobe would later tell me. "I was more than happy to wait it out, acclimatize, and get as much rest as possible. We were in for a long day."

Profile

Charles Crenchaw

Inspired by my newfound knowledge of the Buffalo Soldiers, I began seeking out other compelling stories of African-Americans in the outdoors. When I was invited to write the story of Expedition Denali, I naturally wondered: Who was the first Black person to climb to the top of the highest peak in North America?

In 1963, as Dr. Martin Luther King, Jr., voiced his dream to a rapt crowd on the Washington Mall in Washington, DC, another African-American was forging new ground across the country in Washington State. "I have a dream," King said, "that one day every valley shall be exalted, every hill and mountain shall be made low, the rough places will be made plain, and the crooked places will be made straight." And though his words may have been intended as a metaphor, I like to think that he was speaking not only of equal access to lunch counters, buses, and public places, but also of access to real mountains.

Indeed, in the same issue of *Ebony* magazine that covered Dr. King's March on Washington, a story titled "Weekend Adventurer" featured an up-and-coming African-American climber by the name of Charles Madison Crenchaw, who would summit Mount McKinley just a year later.

Crenchaw was a member of the Seattle Mountaineers and among the first climbers invited by team leader Alvin E. Randall to take part in the thirty-seventh ascent of Mount McKinley's south peak. Though we can't know for certain that he aimed to become the first Black alpinist to reach the highest point in North America, it's hard to believe that Crenchaw wasn't well aware of what his accomplishment might mean during the tumultuous Civil Rights Movement.

Published accounts and journals from expedition members including Crenchaw help draw an account of the ascent. On June 14, 1964, a group of eighteen climbers boarded a train in Anchorage, Alaska, bound for Mount McKinley National Park (the park's name until 1980). The team had originally been composed of a company of six. But as word spread throughout the climbing community of what Randall had in mind, the party "had taken on expedition proportions," Crenchaw wrote in the official report for The Mountaineers, "and turned out to be the largest single group ever to attempt McKinley and the second largest American climbing expedition on record."

The team assembled more than two tons of food and equipment, which was shipped ahead of time to Alaska. Dr. Arthur Harrison of the University of Washington wanted the team to conduct studies on the movement of the Muldrow Glacier, so the climb was granted formal scientific expedition status by the US Department of the Interior. In exchange for surveying the region, establishing benchmarks for the glacier's progress, and collecting flora and geological specimens, the team would receive an extra airdrop of supplies at McGonagall Pass (5,600 feet).

"As we approached the mountain, we were all looking out the window at what would be the altitude of Mt. Rainier (14,411 feet) and saw nothing," Crenchaw would later write. "Then suddenly all heads raised as if on a common lever, 6,000 feet higher; there in the distance stood the top of Denali. No jokes were made, we just quietly settled back in awe. It was huge—most huge! We understood why the Indians named it Denali—The Great One."

Crenchaw's father was a tailor who had served as the Arkansas state chairman of the National Association for the Advancement of Colored People (NAACP) during the 1930s. Though money was scarce during the Great Depression, education was a high priority for the Crenchaw family. His parents worked hard to save up for school, but they could only afford to send one child to college at a time. Charles's older brother Milton attended Tuskegee University. In the lead up to the outbreak of World War II, he joined the famed Tuskegee Airmen during an experiment urged and promoted by First Lady Eleanor Roosevelt to prove that "negroes" could qualify as officers and fliers during World War II. Upon becoming a flight instructor, Milton encouraged his brother Charles to join the unit. Charles Crenchaw excelled and became a master sergeant crew chief in charge of maintenance on a squadron of planes. The Tuskegee Airmen became a valuable and highly competent addition to the Army Air Corps, serving in ferrying and combat units in the European theater.

After military service, Charles Crenchaw attended Morehouse College under the GI Bill. Upon graduation he enrolled in graduate school at the University of Chicago, where he majored in industrial management. Though he was second in his class when he completed his degree, he was advised by the dean of students that, "being a negro," he had little chance of getting a position in his field. Undeterred, Crenchaw searched for a proper job and was hired by the General Cable Company at their plant in New Jersey. A few years later, he left the East Coast to pursue a job offer in California, and eventually landed a position at Boeing in Seattle.

Living so near the Cascade Range, Crenchaw discovered a passion for mountaineering. When later interviewed for *Ebony* magazine, he explained, "I climb because climbing is pleasure for me both physically and mentally. Climbing develops good coordination and balance. It develops good alertness and concentration and builds the body. The climb is exciting and exhilarating. When the summit is achieved, there is a feeling of peacefulness, serenity, and happiness—a oneness with God." Although there are no records of his reaction to getting invited to climb Mount McKinley, it's safe to assume that he considered it the opportunity of a lifetime.

When the team arrived at McKinley Park Station on June 15, they were greeted by a torrential downpour and high winds. After a few hours of rest at the McKinley Park Hotel, Al Randall and an advance team left at 3:00 A.M. on a tour bus, followed by a pickup truck that carried their gear. They traveled about eighty miles to a spot near Wonder Lake, approximately three miles from the Eielson Ranger Station on the high bluffs overlooking the Thorofare River. There the team set up camp and waited for the others to arrive. That afternoon, Randall took a small group out to scout the route near the moraine of the Muldrow Glacier.

A dense fog along the banks of the McKinley River made the going rough. Low visibility and uncertain terrain posed many challenges, as did high water levels that made crossing almost impossible. But four miles downstream, Randall found a favorable spot that would spare the team the misery of having to submerge themselves in the river.

The following day, the entire team set off across the Muldrow Glacier, each carrying eighty- to ninety-pound packs. Three days later, they finally arrived at McGonagall Pass. Higher up on the mountain, the fog was a complete whiteout, unfortunately preventing bush pilot Cliff Hudson from making an airdrop of food and equipment as planned. For two days the party huddled in their tents, eating half rations to conserve food and waiting for the weather to break and fresh supplies to arrive.

The tents, designed for high-altitude environments and freezing temperatures, "took in water like sponges," and it finally became necessary to cut holes in the floor of each one to drain them. On June 20, Hudson took advantage of a brief break in the weather and made his airdrop. But the fog closed in again, forcing him to land and leaving him stranded on the ground for several hours.

Despite the driving rain, the following day Randall led another scouting party up the glacier to establish a route to the Lower Icefall at 7,500 feet. Having last visited the area in 1956, he was surprised to discover that the terrain had changed dramatically. "Where there had been one crevasse then, there were now ten," he later wrote in the trip summary. "At first sight, both the Lower Ice Fall and the Great Ice Fall at 8,500 feet appeared impossible to negotiate."

As Crenchaw and another member of the team set up Camp II on the glacier across from Gunsight Pass at 6,500 feet, they marveled at what they saw before them: "Here we were confronted with our first major obstacle—the Lower Ice Falls, which were crisscrossed with crevasses. One climber said of the icefall, 'It looked as if the gods had been playing tic-tac-toe with ice blocks.' The break-up was horrendous."

For the next several days, the group continued to work in independent teams. Their purpose was to scout safe routes for the others to follow as well as to establish primary campsites where advancing members of the party could rest and recover. Carefully probing his way through the treacherous icefield between the two icefalls, Al Randall set up Camp III at 7,600 feet and Camp IIIA at 8,000 feet. Hudson would make his second airdrop of more than 3,000 pounds of food and equipment there. As the team made their way up to Camp III, Pat Chamay became the first victim of a crevasse. Though he was quickly rescued, the accident brought into sharp relief the unstable nature of their surroundings.

"We rapidly learned that the Muldrow Glacier was very porous, shell-like, and always groaning," Crenchaw wrote in his account of the expedition. "Crevasses were frequently opening, making any deviation from the established route hazardous."

Once the entire team had assembled at Camp III, the weather took another turn for the worse, and the pilot was prevented from making his second equipment drop. Rather than waiting it out in their tents, Randall and a few others attempted to scout a route through the Great Icefall. Just as they entered this particularly dangerous area, a serac believed to weigh at least ten tons cleaved off the mountain, barely missing the climbers as it crashed down in a massive avalanche.

"The mountain was nipping at us," wrote Crenchaw. "Shortly after this, a crevasse some fifteen feet wide opened just after the first rope team had passed."

Despite the glacier's active state, the team managed to ferry loads from the lower camps up to the base of Karstens Ridge at 11,100 feet. The following day, as Pierre Juillerat was leading a group up the mountain, a crevasse opened right beneath him. He fell twenty feet headfirst, toppled over by his heavy pack. Though he too was quickly rescued, the trauma of the fall left him in a state of shock. Fortunately, he sustained only minor cuts and bruises down his back and across his ribs.

The next day, the team relocated all the tents up to Camp IV at Karstens Ridge—with the exception of Juillerat and his rope team, who stayed behind to allow him to recover from his fall. On June 27, a full twelve days after they'd arrived at the mountain, the weather finally cleared and Hudson was able to make his last airdrop. By then, the expedition was five days behind schedule. The team spent the next two days hustling loads from the drop site at 8,000 feet up to the ridge at 11,000 feet. With each round-trip taking as much as ten hours, the climbers were thoroughly exhausted by the time they crawled into their tents at the end of each day. They'd only just settled down to sleep on June 28 when they were awakened at 9:30 P.M. by an earthquake. Though the team suffered no physical ill effects, few slept well that night. Two days later, they would discover that the quake had shaken loose another avalanche from the Harper Icefall that completely obscured the glacier below.

The instability of the glacier and whiteout weather conditions persisted throughout the climb. Over the next several days, the team experienced one harrowing event after another. As Sean Rice and a scouting party made their way up along Karstens Ridge to the base of Browns Tower at 14,600 feet, yet another avalanche nearly swept Rice away. On the same day, Randall fell while shoveling a route through wind-packed snow on a cornice, only managing to avoid a horrific fall of 3,500 feet down onto the Traleika Glacier below by self-arresting with his shovel. Persisting in the face of distressing levels of adversity, the team nonetheless succeeded in establishing Camp V farther up Karstens Ridge at 12,500 feet.

From this point forward, the climb continued with fewer hazards and the team's spirits soared.

"We began in the fog, but as we reached Browns Tower, the mountain was in sunlight," Crenchaw wrote. "From this spot we got our first look at our objective—the South Peak. We were exuberant."

Over the next few days, the team set up Camp VI at 15,500 feet and then a final high camp at 17,700 feet. From there, they would attempt the summit. Three members of the party had taken ill due to fatigue and altitude sickness and decided to stay behind. But Juillerat and his rope team had recovered and rejoined the group by then. So on July 9 at 2:30 A.M., the fifteen remaining members of the team left the high camp and began the long slow climb to the summit. The first team arrived at the top at 11:30 A.M. The group spent a total of three hours on the peak. They made their way up in small groups of three or four. In relatively warm temperatures of twenty degrees above zero, they stood savoring the bright sunshine that came through breaks in the clouds above, despite light snow showers.

"It had been so easy today for most of the climbers that it was hard for them to realize they were actually standing on the summit of Mt. McKinley, the highest point of North America," read the archive log. "Climbers found themselves searching through the clouds for something yet higher."

Crenchaw arrived on the summit at 1:30 P.M. accompanied by Al Randall and his wife, Frances. A photograph of the three climbers together taken by Charles DeHart illustrates the pages of the team's official report.

"We congratulated each other, wiped away a few tears, and then went to work," Crenchaw wrote.

Making the first high-altitude radiotelephone transmission in history, DeHart placed a collect call to his landlady in Seattle before turning the device over to Randall, who called Ome Daiber of the Seattle unit of the Mountain Rescue Council to report the successful summit. He also placed calls to Hudson and the superintendent of Mount McKinley National Park.

The team made it back to high camp by 5:00 P.M. Although they had hoped to make an attempt of Denali's somewhat shorter North Peak, the following morning, heavy snow began to fall and didn't let up for the next two days. Recalling the tragedies that had befallen past expeditions on the descent, the team decided to pack their gear and head for home. Chamay was still in a weakened state, and Crenchaw had a badly infected finger that was not responding well to antibiotics. As soon as the weather permitted on July 12, the entire party descended to the camp on Karstens Ridge.

"We proceeded with care, fully aware that Mt. Koven and Mt. Carpe had been named for climbers who had been swallowed by a crevasse in the Greater Icefall," wrote Norman Benton in his 2003 memoir of the climb. "We were not hankering to have a mountain named for any of us."

Over the next three days, as the team made their way down the mountain, the weather grew progressively warmer, but the going was slow through the Great Icefall and even slower through the Lower Icefall. Several recent avalanches had dislodged massive piles of ice and rock and dramatically changed the landscape from what it had been just two weeks earlier. Crenchaw described this portion of the route as being "like going through the gates of hell." The team finally made it back safely to McGonagall Pass. After being on the move for twenty-two hours on July 14, they were all relieved to be off the Muldrow Glacier.

The team spent one final night by the McKinley River and then began to cross early the next morning. A sudden surge of water swept seven members of the team off their feet, and Chamay was carried downriver almost twenty-five yards before he was able to regain his balance and stand. Fortunately no one was seriously hurt and the only casualty was some lost equipment.

Back out on the highway, they hitched rides back to the bus. When they reached the hotel, Crenchaw received medical attention for his finger. After hot baths and long overdue shaves for the men, the team gathered for a farewell dinner.

"The Mountaineer's McKinley Outing had been a complete success," wrote Crenchaw, "because of careful planning and attention given to each miniscule detail, the close teamwork of the party, and the exceptional leadership of Al Randall."

In all accounts of the expedition, Crenchaw was an equal and well-supported member of the team. The fact that he was a person of color appeared to be wholly irrelevant. His race is mentioned only once at the end among the list of the team's accomplishments. "The First Negro to climb Mt. McKinley—Charles Crenchaw" is included with the same weight and bearing as "The largest number of women to reach the summit—3 in one party" or "the largest number of husband-wife teams—2." These details were recorded for posterity like baseball statistics, worthy of note but hardly a Jackie Robinson moment. Like so many achievements in climbing, the fact of its having occurred would be recognized and celebrated only by those to whom such things truly mattered. Crenchaw, like most climbers, upon his return probably took a day or two off from work before heading back to his job at Boeing with a few new watercooler stories and snapshots.

Crenchaw went on to climb many more mountains over the course of his lifetime and served on the board of directors of the American Alpine Club for many years. He died after a long illness in 1998. Tragically, his accomplishments and legacy went completely unknown and uncelebrated by the next generation of African-American climbers, who might have followed in his footsteps and tackled McKinley themselves if they had only known. Now, in 2013, the members of Expedition Denali aimed to duplicate his feat with similar style, passion, and humility.

CHAPTER FOUR

Unexpected Lessons

THE FOLLOWING MORNING, AFTER A NIGHT OF SUFFICIENTLY COLD temperatures, the Expedition Denali team finally set off from the landing strip on day four of the expedition. They were determined to make a single-carry push to their next campsite at 7,800 feet, a spot at the base of a feature called Ski Hill. A distance of 5.5 miles, it was the longest stretch between any two campsites on the entire trip and included an additional challenge: they would have to transport almost all of the team's food and supplies in one horrendous haul. Fortunately, the terrain itself was quite mild and relatively flat—the team would spend most of the day traversing a massive snowfield with only 600 feet of elevation gain between the two sites.

The main challenge was getting so many climbers organized and on the move up the mountain. Despite the team's enthusiasm, it took effort to rally such a large party with heavy loads and get everyone under way. The expedition had not yet established its rhythm. Though everyone shared a common purpose, they still had to pull together as a team and learn to move as one. In preparation to leave for Camp II, each climber scurried about with more nervous energy than usual:

strapping on snowshoes, applying sunscreen, adjusting the length of trekking poles—a thousand little details insignificant in themselves but collectively critical to the success of their mission. Under Aaron's guidance and leadership, they eventually got their gear together, packed their sleds, and tied into their rope teams.

Together, they carried enough food and fuel for three weeks of travel without resupply. Each person carried more than half their body weight in backpacks stuffed to capacity. The sheer volume of equipment on this carry made for a daunting first day.

Fortunately, the team was able to pull some of their load across the glacier with the help of sleds, allowing them to make better time than the I-Team had anticipated. They managed to cover the distance in about four hours. Hot and sweaty despite the ice all around them and the frigid temperatures, the team was relieved to finally arrive at the relatively level campsite at the base of their first vertical objective, Ski Hill. Though they were exhausted, they were also pleased to have gotten the climb under way and satisfied with the distance they had covered.

On day five of the expedition—counting from when they'd first set foot in Alaska—the team was to carry a portion of their supplies from their camp at 7,800 feet to a point at about 10,000 feet near Kahiltna Pass. The day began with an alpine start at 4:00 A.M. and a hard climb with light packs. Carrying a ration of food and fuel to use at the next campsite, the team deposited their cache, buried it, and headed back to their camp. Having gained 2,200 feet of elevation over a 4.5-mile round-trip, they were beginning to feel the effects of altitude and physical exertion—in addition to physical exhaustion, some experienced mild nausea and dizziness. Others suffered from a throbbing headache or blurry vision.

During the last several hundred feet of the ascent, Scott began having minor pain in his right knee. With no previous injuries, he figured that it was just a little sore from getting worked so thoroughly as he hauled loads up the mountain. "However, on the descent back to 7,800 feet, the pain had become unbearable," Scott told me later. "That minor soreness went from a pain scale of one to two to a seven to eight. It became so unbearable that I had started to drift into thoughts about my impact on the expedition." Scott began to question whether or not he was capable of making the ascent to the summit and wondered what would happen as they climbed higher. Would it be better to quit now?

Many of the climbers likely felt the same way. Mornings that begin before dawn and long days of constant motion can rob the body and spirit of physical energy and enthusiasm. But this kind of self-evaluation and reflection is critical in any expedition. NOLS drills into every participant the importance of self-care above all else. Good awareness of personal limitations that might put your well-being or safety at risk is crucial if you are to protect the integrity of the group as a whole and the success of the expedition.

When they returned to camp that evening, Scott expressed his concerns to Robby, who gave the knee joint a cursory examination to check for swelling, inflammation, and tenderness. He recommended that Scott take some ibuprofen and ice it. Although Scott's knee continued to throb through dinner, the pain subsided shortly after that.

As the team settled in to sleep for the night, Robby came to Scott's tent to check on his condition. After another inspection of the joint, he could find nothing wrong. There was no visible sign of injury and the pain had indeed subsided.

"How old are you, man?" Robby asked.

A bit taken aback by the question, Scott replied dubiously, "Forty-one, why?"

With a broad grin, Robby just nodded and said, "Yep, age, man. You're gonna be OK. You're just getting old."

Scott laughed, but in the many days on the mountain that followed, he would realize that Robby was right.

AS ROBBY RECHORD STRODE BACK TO HIS TENT, HE LOOKED OUT ACROSS the valley below and then up at the high mountains all around him. Dry skin at the corners of his mouth cracked and tingled in the cold as he smiled to himself, reflecting on the exciting road of adventure, risk, and sacrifice that had brought him there. Although he'd been living, working, and playing in the outdoors for decades now, he never failed to marvel at his good fortune.

Robby is tall and lean, with the calm resolve of a man comfortable with who he is and the choices he's made in life. With his surfer-dude uniform of a Baja-hoodie, poorly cultivated growth of facial hair, and long mane of dark brown dreadlocks with streaks of blond always tucked under a sun visor or a bandana, he projects a distinctly casual appearance.

But it would be both unfair and unwise to draw any conclusions from that. Behind the sunglasses and toothy grin is a sharp mind, a warm compassionate heart, and a gentle spirit finely tuned to those things in life that truly matter. As a guide and field instructor with NOLS for almost twenty years, Robby has exhaustive experience and expertise in both backcountry skiing and whitewater boating. With a particular interest in avalanche safety and prevention, he was an advocate of best practices in the snow-covered mountains of his home in Idaho, where he was the program supervisor at the NOLS branch in Teton Valley. Evangelistic about backcountry safety, he is known among his peers as the "Right Reverend Robby Rip-Cord of the First Church of the Open Slopes."

Robby also has the distinction of being one of three African-American instructors employed at NOLS. In an organization with eight hundred instructors worldwide, that's a remarkably small number. Though NOLS has several Black staff members from Kenya and Tanzania, such as I-Team member KG (James Kagambi), only fellow field instructors Philip Henderson and Cliff DeBride hail from the New World. But Robby is the first to tell you that he never wanted to be known as a Black skier or a Black mountaineer. "I just want to have my shit tight," he's fond of saying, "and do the best I can at whatever I do."

Raised in Chicago by a single mother, Robby was fortunate to have the benefit of positive role models who shaped both his character and his appreciation for the natural world. Introduced to the outdoors by his grandfather, a retired electrician who lived outside of the city in Robins, Illinois, Robby spent much of his youth exploring the green spaces that dotted the urban landscape of Chicago.

Robby spent his summers in Robins, where he worked pickup electrical jobs with his grandfather around town for a little cash. After work, the two would enjoy the late afternoon and early evenings fishing on the lakes of the Cook County Forest Preserve, a sporadically green landscape along the edges of Chicago's inner city. Though it consisted of little more than a single square mile of small forests surrounded on all sides by busy highways, to Robby's young eyes, it was a haven. On those summer afternoons, the outdoors—no matter how small—was a peaceful oasis where Robby and his grandfather sat for hours fishing and listening to the Lawrence Welk Show on the radio.

"I'd say my grandpa was my best friend," Robby said. "Until I realized that it wasn't cool to have your grandpa as your best friend."

Robby attended De La Salle, a racially diverse Catholic high school in Chicago. There he received a solid primary education and learned a great deal about how to work and live with different kinds of people. The multiethnic education he received would serve him in good stead, allowing him to function and thrive in almost any social environment. It also gave him the freedom to choose any course of life his heart desired.

"My mom always said that I needed to know how to operate in this world as a Black man. You got to be bilingual," Robby said. "You have to be able to talk trash on the streets and speak the King's English when it is time to do that."

In 1989, Robby left Chicago to attend college in New Orleans. There he picked up mountain biking, riding the bumpy trails of the Monkey Hill trash heap in City Park. Quick to pick up the skills necessary to negotiate the tight corners and steep terrain of this small but challenging course, Robby soon realized he wanted more. After a single visit to the Rocky Mountains out west, he decided to transfer to Colorado College, where he could thoroughly indulge his passion for mountain bikes. As soon as he arrived, he immediately took up rock climbing.

What Robby enjoyed most about both sports was the experience of relating to his body in a different way. In mountain biking, he loved using his arms and legs for locomotion, but he was also intrigued by the idea of spinning the gears of a bike and using his hips, knees, and abdominal muscles to negotiate different obstacles and the changing surface of the trail as he charged through it. In climbing, as he gained experience, he learned that rock climbing wasn't about brute strength, but rather about balance. Most importantly, he discovered the importance of working *with* the stone features rather than trying to overcome them.

Pretty much hooked, Robby dove headfirst into the Colorado adventure scene. As soon as the weather turned cold, he took up skiing. The powdery snow of the Rocky Mountains was nothing like the alternately icy or slushy conditions he'd experienced growing up in the Midwest. However, in spite of his enthusiasm for skiing, as a cash-strapped college student, he had difficulty acquiring the gear he needed to take up the sport in a big way.

So he improvised. Robby's first pair of skis came out of a dumpster. His first pair of boots were donated by a friend. Someone else gave him an old pair of used rain pants. Another gave him a jacket. As soon as Robby expressed an interest in learning to ski, his friends came out of the woodwork to help cobble together all the equipment he needed to hit the slopes.

Throughout that first season, he skied as many days as he could, all while attending classes and waiting tables in restaurants. Despite his mismatched clothes and ill-fitting equipment, he was living an active life he truly loved. The following summer, he wanted to up his game with better gear, so he did what most young men do when they want something: He asked his mom. When he presented her with his request, she turned to him and said, "Well, I want a deck on the house."

Back home for the summer, Robby worked as a fill-in janitor for Chicago Public Schools, where his mother worked as an administrator. He spent his evenings building his mom's new deck, and his days mopping floors and scrubbing toilets. By the end of the summer, he'd earned enough money to buy himself a brand new pair of backcountry telemark skis.

Equipped with proper gear, Robby honed his alpine skills on the backcountry slopes of Colorado. When he graduated from college in 1994, he moved with a group of friends to Jackson, Wyoming, to devote himself to skiing in earnest. He had a couple of pairs of skis at that point and a few thousand dollars saved up. He decided he could either spend most of his money on a ski pass or buy a beacon and shovel for three or four hundred bucks and dedicate the entire winter to skiing in the backcountry.

Opting for plan B, Robby invested in some technical equipment to allow him to backcountry ski in the bowls behind the posh resorts of Jackson Hole. He shared a house with six other people, worked a variety of part-time jobs waiting tables, and lived sparingly on whatever cheap food he could scrounge up from the local supermarket. It was a classic ski-bum existence.

Come summer, Robby discovered the joys of whitewater kayaking. As melting winter snow filled the many tributaries near Jackson to overflowing, he once again built himself a kit of used equipment and learned the skills necessary to paddle the raging rapids of the Snake River. After a few seasons of recreational boating, Robby left restaurant work behind and became a professional river guide for Mad River Boat Trips.

Robby was thoroughly embedded in Jackson's adventure community. Now twenty-eight, he and a crew of fellow river guides would arrive at the boathouse every morning at 7:00 A.M. After assembling their gear, they'd run a whitewater raft full of delighted, screaming clients down the Snake River. Returning to the boathouse in the evening around 6:00 P.M., Robby and the crew would grab their personal boats and set off to paddle the river on their own. The long summer days were full of fun and adventure, and Robby loved every minute of it.

By the following year, however, day rafting was beginning to get old. Robby was approaching thirty and realized that there was little future for him in hanging out with twenty-somethings who had a completely different set of personal and professional priorities. Deciding that he wanted to get into multiday guiding, he began to look around at his options. With several friends now working for NOLS, Robby thought it would be a good idea to take some advanced waterman training, and maybe even a certification course to become an instructor. Knowing that NOLS was one of the most prestigious institutions of outdoor education, he figured that it was his best chance to take his skills—and ambitions—to a much higher level. He signed up for a whitewater training course—and never left.

Discovering he was in his element, Robby went on to work several courses for NOLS and eventually earned a full-time position. He's been there ever since, always making sure that everyone has their "shit tight" and is prepared to do the very best they could do.

But as part of Expedition Denali, Robby had to admit he had certain reservations. Thinking back to the outfitting bay at the Farm, he remembered all of that brand new gear everyone had. These climbers didn't have ill-fitting hand-me-downs or gear scrounged from a dumpster. "No one ever gave me a free trip to Denali," he muttered to himself.

He set aside any feelings of resentment, however, with a shrug. These were good people on a solid mission to help kids like he used to be to have opportunities in life. Robby knew better than most that it really doesn't matter how anyone arrives on the mountain. Black or white, rich or poor, it's the mountain that decides whether or not you're going to stay.

THE NEXT MORNING, DAY SIX, THE TEAM ONCE AGAIN WOKE WELL before dawn and fueled up on rations of hot oatmeal, nuts, and dried fruit in anticipation of the hard day ahead. After packing away their tents and sleeping bags, they began the arduous trip up to the next site at 11,000 feet. This portion of the climb was tough for even the strongest climbers among them. While the earlier hauls had been over relatively gentle and steady ground, the terrain now began to include some appreciable hills and steep inclines as they made their way to the top of Ski Hill. Although the route still didn't necessitate a lot of technical skill, it would prove to be an unforgiving test of their individual strength and endurance. Despite months of training, very little could have prepared them for what lay ahead.

Even with a good portion of their supplies cached at 10,000 feet, their loads remained heavy, making the climb extremely difficult. In addition to the challenging terrain, this stretch was more than a little nerve-racking. Surrounded by a glittering expanse of ice and deep snow, the path snaked along a crevasse field next to an avalanche slope and an icefall. The camp was located right in the middle of this hazardous area, and it required no small amount of ingenuity and extremely careful thought for the I-Team to select a safe campsite that posed the least risk of crevasses or an avalanche.

The camp at 11,000 feet was set in a wide basin with two mountain slopes on either side. The icefalls that ringed the steep walls of rock above contained massive slabs of ice that could easily melt in the unusually warm weather and tumble down into the valley where the camp was located. The glacier underfoot was slowly on the move and riddled with cracks of varying depth and width that were impossible to see beneath a layer of snow. Before the party entered the campsite—before anyone even untied from their ropes—three of the climbers still on belay used long metal poles to probe a wide area of ground for crevasses. They probed and cleared a patch of snow on the glacier with enough room for each of the rope teams to pitch their tents, establish a kitchen for cooking, and create a common toilet for everyone to share. Once the camp parameter had been clearly marked with flags indicating where it was safe to walk, each climber entered the camp one at a time. Only then did they take themselves off belay and untie their ropes.

The hazards in this area put into context the sheer magnitude of their undertaking. All of them felt a new surge of pressure as they stepped into camp. In a way, it was the first time that the mountain—and the scale of the challenge they had taken on—became fully real to them. From this point on, they were all at very serious risk of injury or even death if anyone should forget, for even a moment, where they were.

As the team set up camp at 11,000 feet, an accident brought this new reality into sharp focus. While organizing gear, Tyrhee noticed a haul sled suddenly come loose and start slipping downhill. Without thinking, he ran after the sled as it sped down the icy slope, back the way they had come. In a flying leap, he dove after it. Though he managed to stop its downward slide, the impact of his body against the ice and weight of the sled left him writhing in pain. Tyrhee thought he might have dislocated his shoulder. In chasing after a sled through an active crevasse field, Tyrhee not only put his own safety at risk but the safety of everyone on the team. And by possibly dislocating his shoulder, he set in motion a decision-making process that might disrupt the entire expedition.

NOLS has very stringent standard field practices set up by the group's medical advisory board and risk management director. If it's determined that a participant has a true separation or dislocation, that person must be evacuated for closer examination. There was suddenly a good chance that Tyrhee would be heading home. Although Tyrhee didn't want that to happen, he started to question whether he might be a risk to the team if he stayed on.

As the others set up camp, the instructors examined Tyrhee's arm and tested his mobility, strength, and level of pain. The following day, as most of the team headed back down the mountain to retrieve their cache at 10,000 feet, Aaron stayed behind with Tyrhee and deliberated over what to do next. Aaron tried to get more clarity on the young man's original declaration. "What makes you feel like it's dislocated?" Aaron asked him.

Though still in pain, Tyrhee believed that he wasn't as badly injured as he had first thought. But what was best for the group and the expedition was also foremost in his mind. Would he be able to perform as part of a rope team? With a damaged shoulder, his ability to execute a self-arrest in the event of a fall would be compromised. His injury not only put him at risk but also jeopardized his role as rescuer should he have to come to the assistance of someone else.

By the time everyone had returned from picking up the cache, Tyrhee knew his fate as a member of Expedition Denali was no longer in his hands. After much debate with his teammates and the instructors, Tyrhee was prepared to do whatever they thought best for the success of the expedition—even if that meant being taken off the mountain. But in the end, the others on the team all made it clear that they would look after him. No one wanted Tyrhee to go home.

"Everyone pushed for me to stay and really didn't want me gone," Tyrhee said. "I was really torn and was so upset it happened. However, it made me realize how important being a part of that expedition was for me."

Tyrhee ultimately got medical clearance from the instructors and stayed, but for the rest of the trip, he had a much more profound respect for the magnitude of their undertaking. He had never over the course of his young life been faced with having to consider the consequences of his own decisions in a situation where the risk of loss was so great. And though he was relieved to have the support and encouragement of his teammates, he would never forget how his actions, no matter how insignificant they might seem, could directly affect the outcome of the entire expedition. In grappling with his thoughts and emotions around the incident, the youngest member of the team experienced an unexpected opportunity for growth and maturity.

Profile

Sophia Danenberg

Having learned a hard lesson from his experience at 11,000 feet, Tyrhee will likely think twice before chasing a runaway sled down an icy snowfield again. There are many things that only time in the mountains can teach a new climber. In Robby, Shobe, Adina, and Aaron, Tyrhee has a solid corps of mentors to literally show him the ropes on a major expedition. It's also through their example that he might realize all that a life of adventure has to offer.

Tyrhee and other young people of color can certainly be inspired and encouraged by the achievements of climbers from all walks of life. But there's something to be said for the value of heroes with whom they share a similar background and heritage, people who have experienced many of the same challenges, endured the same hardships, and celebrated the same triumphs. If you are young and Black American, Black role models make a difference.

Sophia Danenberg, an accomplished climber and avid supporter of Expedition Denali, is just such a role model. A professional woman of high aspirations, she has created a lifestyle for herself that makes it possible for her to make mountaineering a priority. Her job as an international policy analyst at Boeing calls for a lot of travel, a perk that enables her to climb an almost dizzying number of mountains all over the world. Through years of experience—she has successfully reached the rocky summits of Rainier, Ama Dablam, Tasman, Grand Teton,

Baker, and Denali—she has learned to have confidence in her abilities, tempered by a humility that only time in the mountains can teach.

Although she is just over five feet tall and slightly built, Sophia's small stature belies her physical strength. Her straight onyx-colored hair reveals her mother's Japanese heritage, and her African-American father lent her complexion a warm milk chocolate brown. Raised in a family of modest privilege and high expectations, Sophia has charged through life with the talent and discipline to rise to the top of her profession while still enjoying a variety of personal passions, which include a love of international travel and a taste for adventure.

Ever keen to add to her already accomplished mountaineering resume, Sophia had planned on a trip to Cho Oyu, the world's sixth highest mountain, in 2006. It would have been the latest in a long career spent ticking off one lofty summit after another in the manner so common to alpinists. On the trip she hoped to climb with Tashi Tenzing, the grandson of Tenzing Norgay, who in 1953 with Sir Edmund Hillary, was the first to summit Mount Everest, the world's highest peak.

But while arranging her travel plans, the conversation took a surprising turn. By the end of the call, Sophia had decided to climb not Cho Oyu but Everest instead.

"The tour company director thought I could climb with their unguided program since I had done nearly all my climbing up to that point unguided and had climbed Ama Dablam the previous season in a similar fashion," Sophia told me. "It only cost half what I had heard Everest normally cost, so it made it more reasonable."

As an "unguided" expedition, this journey to the summit of Everest was meant for experienced climbers. Unlike many trips led by modern outfitters that require only that a person be in good physical shape, this trip was for mountaineers who knew what they were doing on a

26,000-foot summit. Sophia and eight other climbers were provided only with a tent site at base camp and at each of the four camps on the southern route, two Sherpa climbing partners, weather reports, food, and canisters of oxygen.

The Sherpas were there primarily for companionship and as an emergency measure—so that the climbers wouldn't find themselves utterly alone on the mountain with no possibility of rescue should something go wrong. They weren't guides and they weren't prepared to make any decisions regarding the climb itself. Sophia would be pretty much on her own when it came time to decide when to head up the mountain and, even more importantly, when to come back down. She wouldn't have had it any other way.

Sophia was one of few women at base camp. Given her size, the Sherpas and the other climbers were impressed by her ability to walk long distances under the weight of a very heavy pack. "Hey, this woman is really strong," she recalls hearing them say. "You look Nepalese, only with better hair."

After spending several weeks acclimating to the altitude, she set out from Everest Base Camp with her two Sherpa companions, a pair of brothers named Pa Nuru and Mingma Tshiring. Sophia's primary partner, Pa Nuru, climbed with her, while Mingma carried bottles of oxygen for Sophia and the other unguided client who was ascending then. Her small team carefully negotiated the arduous passage over the Khumbu Icefall—an undulating field of vertical pillars and treacherous crevasses—with trekking poles and crampons. They crossed the sturdy ladder bridges that had been set up so that climbers could traverse the deep canyons carved into the landscape like violent slashes of a giant's ax. As they teetered precariously over each metal rung, Sophia stared down into a blue-black abyss that appeared to be all but bottomless.

Even under the weight of her heavily laden pack, she kept an even pace with her companions, and eventually made it up to Camp I at 19,500 feet.

The next day, they continued steadily up the mountain, straining against appreciably less oxygen with every foot of altitude they gained. At Camp II, feeling strong and confident in her chances for success, Sophia committed to making a summit attempt. The following morning, she and her companions pushed on steadily to Camp III at the base of Everest's neighbor, Lhotse, a lesser-known but equally beautiful peak.

As they worked their way up to Camp IV at 26,000 feet, they entered what is known as the death zone, so named both because of the profound lack of oxygen, too little for humans to tolerate for long even with supplemental oxygen, and the ever-present threat of bad weather. Although high winds and blowing snow were a constant, a window of clear skies remained open for the time being. However, conditions had begun to worsen lower down on the mountain, and Sophia wondered if it was a good idea to continue on.

From Camp IV, high above the clouds, she could see for miles across the Khumbu Valley. From a vantage point at 27,500 feet called the Balcony, she told herself that she would one day visit at least a few of those distant peaks, which loomed so large in her vision that she felt she could reach out and touch them. But there was little time to focus on future plans just then. In the clouds below, she discerned flashes of lightning in a violently churning storm that might overtake her and dash her summit plans. Unsure what to do, Sophia turned to Pa Nuru and asked him if he thought the weather would hold—should they go on?

"It's your decision," he said.

Around 11:00 P.M. on May 18, Sophia and the other unguided climber decided to leave Camp IV with the Sherpas and make a bid for the summit. A few other parties had left earlier that evening, but she and her companions soon caught up to them and then passed them. They carried on ever higher into the night, their steps lit only by headlamps. The steep terrain eventually proved too much for her fellow climber, who turned back and returned to camp with his Sherpa climber. Although she still had her companions, Sophia suddenly felt very alone.

"I thought everyone except us had turned around," she told me later. "I thought we were the only people on the mountain. It never crossed my mind that we could be going so much faster that they could be that far behind us."

She made her way across the long precarious ridge that joins the peaks of Everest and Lhotse like the spinal vertebrae of a dragon's back. Then she ascended the famed Hillary Step and reached the summit ridge. Studying the final stretch, she was elated to have made such excellent progress. It hadn't been easy, but she had experienced no complications, and for that she was grateful.

Sophia reached the summit of Everest on May 19, 2006, at 7:00 A.M. Because she was at least two hours ahead of any other climbers that day, she had the peak all to herself. Aside from a bit of frostbite on her cheeks and a touch of bronchitis that made breathing even more difficult, she was in good health and fine spirits. As she stood there taking in the view, one of her Sherpa companions took her photograph—a tiny woman with a broad smile standing on top of the world.

Though it was not widely reported in the media, Sophia Danenberg was the first African-American to make it to the top of Mount Everest. It was a great accomplishment to be sure, but with so many people successfully making the climb year after year (477 people made it to the top in 2006), the exploits of a single alpinist often go unnoticed. Even

Sophia failed to find anything particularly newsworthy in her having climbed the highest peak on the planet.

"I just look at myself as a pretty average amateur mountaineer," Sophia said. "The things I climb are the things that people climb. Some are technical, sure, but nothing spectacular."

Modern mountaineering—unlike many social institutions through the last century—has no history of racial discrimination. While professional sports, such as Major League Baseball (which wasn't integrated until 1947), actively prohibited the participation of African-Americans, climbing has been open to everyone since its inception. To name just one example, the American Alpine Club has only ever restricted membership based on the skills and abilities of individuals seeking admittance. In fact, according to club librarians, the signatories of the original charter in 1902 included two women.

So as an athlete with no sponsors to please, Sophia never felt compelled to boast about her "first ascent." As it turned out, she was uncomfortable even discussing it.

"I climb because I like to climb. And to have my birth bring more significance to it is tough for me," she said. "I know that it has significance for other people, but I struggle with it in my head. It's almost embarrassing."

The mountain and weather and avalanches don't know or even care what race you are, how short or tall, or whether you're a man or woman. There on the mountain, you're just a climber. And like most climbers, Sophia aspired to be recognized exclusively for her mountaineering skills. As a role model, she is a fine example for anyone—of any color—to follow. And for her to reach one of the highest goals in climbing with little attention paid to her race was, in her mind, a testament to how far we've come.

CHAPTER FIVE

Windy Corner

THE EXPEDITION DENALI TEAM SPENT A TOTAL OF THREE DAYS AT 11,000 feet. Although they took the opportunity to rest and acclimate, they also completed the arduous task of moving their cache to a location at 13,000 feet, which was located near a particularly treacherous—and infamous—section on the route called Windy Corner.

In 2005 a group of climbers on a guided trip with the Alaska Mountaineering School (AMS) had suffered serious injuries and one fatality due to rockfall in this area. On their descent after a successful summit the previous day, three four-man rope teams made the traverse below the headwall that leads to the West Buttress of Denali at the top of a feature called Squirrel Hill. The most difficult part of this transition is marked by a sudden turn off a south-facing slope enveloped in shadows and protected from the wind to a westerly wall thoroughly bathed in sunlight and bearing the full brunt of every northern breeze, no matter how slight. Subject to repeated and extreme variations in temperature—from freezing cold to swelteringly hot—Windy Corner is highly susceptible to a sudden and catastrophic avalanche of falling rocks, ice, and snow.

In the *American Alpine Journal*'s report on the accident, the twelve climbers had only just rounded Windy Corner when a thunderous crack alerted them to danger above. Though they initially believed that they had gotten beyond the danger zone, they found themselves in a horrific rockslide moments later. Three of the climbers on the first rope team were struck by falling debris. The fourth immediately assumed a self-arrest position and succeeded in breaking their fall, but the three who'd fallen were all seriously injured.

An AMS guide who'd witnessed the fall phoned for help. But there was no response from the ranger outposts at Advance Base Camp or the landing strip at 7,200 feet. The guide finally managed to reach a National Park Service ranger who contacted his fellow guides at AMS headquarters in Talkeetna. A rescue helicopter was sent immediately.

Meanwhile a rescue team was formed at Advance Base Camp (also called 14 Camp because of its position at 14,200 feet) and carefully set off for Windy Corner. Although they all acted quickly, one of the climbers had already died from his injuries by the time the rescue team finally arrived. The two remaining injured climbers survived but sustained serious fractures that included a broken femur, several broken ribs, and a ruptured disc.

Though in 2013 nothing so tragic had occurred since, climbing guides on Denali continued to exercise extreme caution when negotiating Windy Corner. It's common practice to cache supplies just beyond this major rockfall area so that there are few significant obstacles between the climbers and their food on the descent in the event of bad weather. But given the particularly warm climbing season, the danger zone extended much farther than in years past.

A group photo at 14 Camp of all the people of color on the mountain during the 2013 season, including the Expedition Denali team. *From left to right, back row:* Adina Scott, Ryan Hudson, Rosemary Saal, Billy Long, Stephen Shobe, Ryan Mitchell, Tyrhee Moore, Erica Wynn, James "KG" Kagambi. *Front row:* Robby ReChord, Scott Briscoe, Madhu Chikkaraju, Stephen DeBerry, Philip Henderson. (Photo courtesy of Hudson Henry)

Rosemary Saal, Erica Wynn, and Adina Scott at 14 Camp (Photo courtesy of Hudson Henry)

Rosemary Saal (Photo courtesy of Hudson Henry)

Billy Long (Photo courtesy of Hudson Henry)

Tyrhee Moore (Photo courtesy of Hudson Henry)

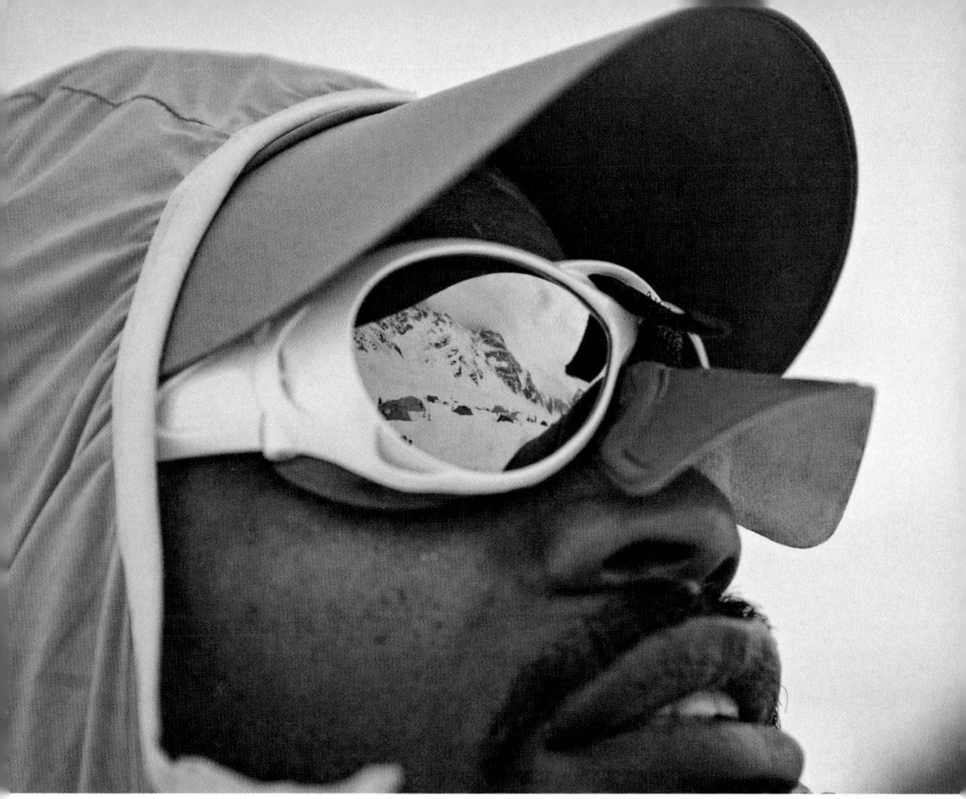

Stephen DeBerry (Photo courtesy of Hudson Henry)

Erica Wynn (Photo courtesy of Hudson Henry)

Ryan Mitchell (Photo courtesy of Hudson Henry)

Sophia Danenberg (Photo courtesy of Sophia Danenberg)

Shelton Johnson (Photo courtesy of Shelton Johnson)

Ryan Hudson (Photo courtesy of Max Lowe)

Charles Crenchaw (Photo courtesy of Dee Molenaar)

Scott Briscoe (Photo courtesy of Hudson Henry)

Madhu Chikkaraju, one of the team's instructors, climbing the headwall's fixed lines. (Photo courtesy of Hudson Henry)

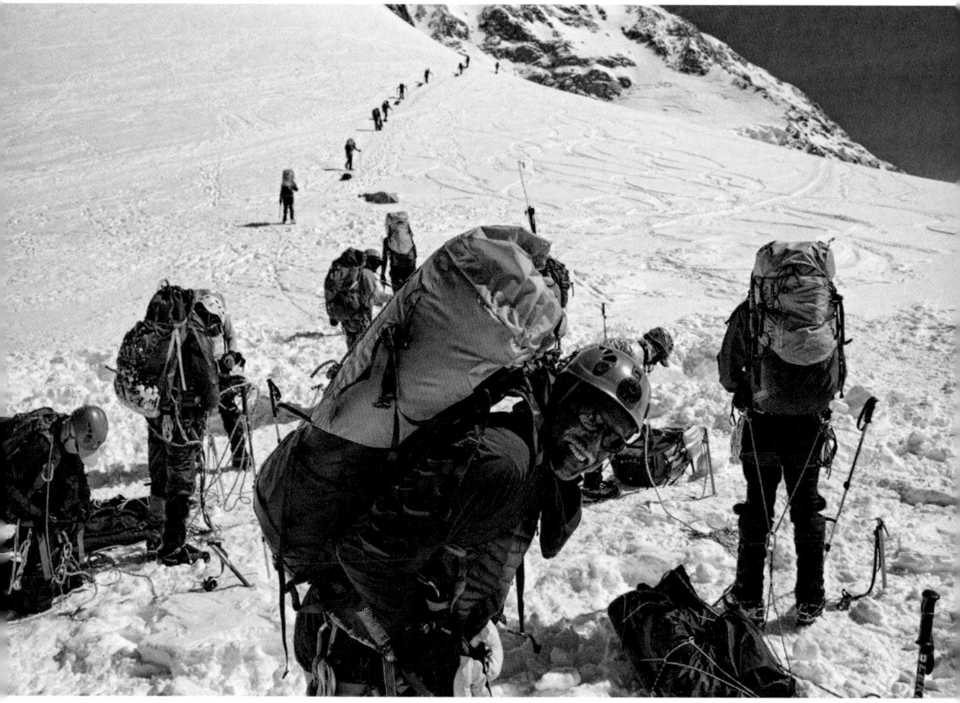

Stephen Shobe at Windy Corner (Photo courtesy of Hudson Henry)

Expedition Denali approaches high camp at 17,200 feet. (Photo courtesy of Hudson Henry)

Robby ReChord (Photo courtesy of Hudson Henry)

Aaron Divine (Photo courtesy of Hudson Henry)

Kai Lightner and Connie Lightner
(Photo courtesy of James Edward Mills)

Matthew Henson (Photo courtesy of matthewhenson.org, a free public service provided by Verne Robinson)

Barbara Hillary (Photo courtesy of Barbara Hillary)

Stephen Shobe (Photo courtesy of Hudson Henry)

Adina Scott (Photo courtesy of Hudson Henry)

Dawn backlights Denali. (Photo courtesy of Hudson Henry)

ON THE MORNING EXPEDITION DENALI WOULD CARRY THEIR FIRST cache load up to Windy Corner, the weather appeared to be in a cooperative mood, with clear skies and very little wind. But such good conditions also meant they would have a lot of company, as teams from other parties hustled up and down the route to take full advantage of the favorable window of opportunity. By Denali standards, it looked like it was going to be a very busy day.

After getting off to a brisk start, the team took a break on a narrow ridge before tackling the part of Windy Corner most exposed to a fall. Everyone took advantage of the moment to adjust their layering systems, make sure they had everything they needed, and drink some water. The section before them consisted of a long narrow path across a precariously steep field of snow. Polished to a smooth, solid sheet of ice by unrelenting gusts of wind, the trail offered no protection for several hundred yards. Even crampons offered only scant comfort—it was better simply not to fall. Everyone knew from all that they had heard about this place that, once they turned Windy Corner, they would bear the full brunt of the sun, violent wind, and risk of rockfall. Once they started, there would be no stopping until they were safely on the other side of this treacherous stretch.

Around 11:00 A.M., the team started walking again. Within a few rope lengths of the most dangerous area, a cascade of falling rocks came tumbling down.

"There was a group of Russian climbers coming down through Windy Corner, and there was one other group led by AAI [American Alpine Institute] that had passed us right at the end of our break," Aaron said. "We coordinated with them to go ahead of us because they were a smaller group and could make it around the corner faster. The rocks fell between the AAI group and the Russian group."

Some of the rocks were the size of an ice chest. Had anyone been directly in their path, the rockfall could easily have resulted in a tragedy similar to the one that occurred in 2005. As the AAI group continued on past Windy Corner toward 14 Camp and the Russian climbers made their way down toward the Kahiltna Glacier, the Expedition Denali team decided on a change of plans. Instead of depositing their cache on the far side of the rockfall area, as was customary, they dropped their supplies before reaching it and then turned back.

After a long and harrowing day of ferrying their loads, the team settled in back at camp, hungry for their evening meal. But it was here that an odd quirk of group dynamics came unexpectedly into play. During more than a week together on the mountain, team members had established a rhythm and grown accustomed to the long days of hauling their gear across treacherous crevasse fields. Despite a general sense of exhaustion, everyone felt comfortable in their community of nylon tents, and because of that they had grown relaxed in their routine. That night they forgot a key chore that would have serious consequences the next day.

Scott flexed his knee as he crawled out the narrow doorway of the home he shared with DeBerry and Erica. He tested the knee with a few short squats and a full body stretch, his arms raised high overhead as he stood on his toes. It didn't seem to be as sore as it had been a few days earlier. After a short nap, he roused himself to help cook dinner. But he was pleased to see that the evening meal was already under way.

DeBerry sat on a square block of snow stirring a steaming pot. The gas jets of the stove roared beneath the sound of a thick bubbling liquid. As Scott drew closer, the smell of garlic and onions filled the air along with the sweet scent of some kind of herb—oregano? Corkscrew tendrils of rotini pasta were bubbling away in a red sauce of sundried tomatoes and olive oil. Flakes of cheddar cheese melted slowly into the mix as DeBerry carved off slivers from an orange brick in a ziplock plastic bag.

"Dude, that looks amazing," Scott said. "I'm starving. Let me get my cup."

Jogging back to his tent, Scott spread the word to the rest of team. "Dinner's ready!"

Heads poked out of doorways and everyone hustled over to where DeBerry sat cooking. Ladling out portions into each insulated cup, the businessman served up his creation to a small crowd of satisfied customers who gobbled down every bite before the chill air stole the food's heat.

While Rosemary and Tyrhee cleaned the large cooking pots, Adina and Billy packed away the supplies. All nine climbers now shared the duties of preparing their meals. Typically, these tasks were divided up by tent assignments, and each miniteam of three shared a stove, bottles of fuel, and turns as camp chef. But as friends working together, the climbers had centralized a few of their responsibilities. This approach reduced the burden on everyone and gave them more time to relax and recover. Unfortunately, though everyone volunteered to take on many of the important tasks, no one thought about preparing enough water so that there would be plenty for everyone.

It takes a great deal of effort to create every drop of water consumed on a high-altitude mountaineering expedition. Every member of the team carried with them almost a gallon of stove fuel meant for the sole purpose of melting snow. And it's each person's individual responsibility to make sure that he or she has enough water to make it through every day of the trip. When water runs short, the result isn't merely thirst. The climbers' ability to perform at their peak becomes severely compromised and puts everyone in danger. In the excessive heat of long days spent ascending the mountain, everyone on the team was at risk of extreme dehydration. Dizziness, discomfort, exhaustion, diminished reflexes, confusion, and lethargy are only a few of the symptoms caused by dehydration. In many ways, the expedition's success hinged on having an adequate and steady water supply.

"Technically everyone is responsible for making their own water, and when we combined our cooking groups, I think everyone was counting on someone else to take care of it," Scott later admitted. "So when we needed it most, it just wasn't there."

By the time they set off from their 11,000-foot camp the following morning, several members of the team were carrying well below their full water capacity. Heading to 14 Camp, the climbers had to cover more than two miles with an elevation gain of 3,000 feet. The challenging ascent and rising temperatures throughout the morning made the going hot and sweaty.

The mountaineers were also buffeted by a persistent gust that dramatically lowered the temperature of the air. In the mountain's shadow, well out of the sun's warmth, Adina suddenly grew chilled. She drew the insulating layer of her puffy jacket just a bit tighter beneath her Gore-Tex shell in an effort to keep the cold at bay. But just a few minutes later, she turned Windy Corner and the blazing sun appeared. Even though they'd been led to expect this sudden change in temperature, it was nevertheless a shock to their already exhausted bodies. Now in the heart of the most dangerous part of the rockfall area, they had no choice but to keep moving. Since they couldn't stop to remove layers of clothing, they continued to lose their bodies' moisture to perspiration. Already low on water, they couldn't even slow down to drink what little they had. And as they picked up their pace to get out of harm's way, everyone grew even hotter.

Although guidebooks describe this area of rockfall danger as being relatively short, because of the unseasonably warm weather, the team was exposed for much longer than they expected. A passage that should have taken only twenty minutes stretched on for almost an hour. Thirsty and exhausted and hoping for relief, they trudged on.

Shobe slowed for a moment, just long enough to clear the fog from his sunglasses. The perspiration from his damp face radiated steam that wafted upward, only to get trapped between his helmet and balaclava. With every exhalation, his body expelled more of its precious moisture. He had little water left in his pack to replace it and was rapidly becoming thoroughly dehydrated. He nonetheless continued to move forward. Increasingly exhausted, Shobe concentrated all his attention on putting one foot in front of the other, one foot in front of the other.

Ahead of him, the other members of his rope team were confronting another steep incline. As they negotiated the narrow trail, the sun beat down with the ferocity of a sledgehammer. And as the temperature slowly increased, rocks overhead began to loosen along with massive slabs of ice and snow. Just as 14 Camp came into view, a huge avalanche swept across the mountain. Though it was out of range of the climbers, it was nonetheless unnerving. Exhausted as they were, few of the climbers would have had the energy to execute an effective self-arrest to save themselves or another member of their rope team. When the teams finally arrived at Advance Base Camp, they were collectively spent. The combination of the difficult terrain, stress of potential rockfall, and thirst had taken a lot out of everyone.

Although Aaron had seen that many of the climbers were struggling, it wasn't until later that evening when they met as a team that he discovered that most everyone had left camp that morning with less water than they should have. Their system of sharing the preparation of food had been their undoing. With no one designated to prepare water for everyone, the result was a shortage, and the deficit was harmful. It underscored how a seemingly mundane task—melting the day's drinking water—can have a tremendous impact on the success of an expedition. The group believed they were working effectively as a team by collectively cooking their food; in reality, their effort caused confused priorities and undermined their group success.

Despite their exhaustion and frayed nerves, the team's flagging spirits were revived by what they saw as they arrived at 14 Camp. A small city of nylon tents with groups of people in various states of activity, it had an almost festive air about it. And with good reason: at 14,200 feet, they were now within striking range of the summit.

Wisps of steam rose up from kitchen sites where cookstoves were boiling water for drinking or a hot meal. Young men on skis and snowboards carved turns off the slopes of the headwall and jumped recklessly from icy ramps over deep crevasses. After working so hard to get there, it was evidently time to play. And with the most difficult part of the mountain now behind them, everyone appeared ready to focus on what lay ahead. Rosemary told me later about the sensational view: "You can see mountains for miles and miles and miles," she said. "If you can see them now, you could only imagine what it's going to be like on the summit."

Located on a glacial plateau at 14,200 feet, 14 Camp, or Advance Base Camp, consisted of a flat expanse of ice surrounded by high peaks. It offered not only an unobstructed view of Mount Hunter and Mount Foraker to the south, but also the team's first view of Denali's summit. Though they would still have to retrieve and carry their cache from the other side of Windy Corner the following day, the group basked in the pleasure of being on safe ground. And as they gradually grew accustomed to their surroundings, they discovered an aspect of mountaineering most of them had never experienced.

A gathering point for climbers from all over the world, 14 Camp was filled with hundreds of mountaineers who were taking several days to recharge their energy and enthusiasm before embarking on their final push to the summit. The Expedition Denali team enjoyed a bit of celebrity status, as several of the other climbers were familiar with their initiative and were excited to see them doing so well.

Among the many climbers the team encountered here was Alex Straus. On a guided trip of his own, he was thrilled to be reunited with Billy, DeBerry, and Scott. It had been almost a year since Alex was rescued from a crevasse on the Matanuska Glacier. He briefly met up with his former companions as he made his way back down the mountain after summiting two days earlier. "I will never forget those guys," he told me.

Tyrhee was especially pleased with the attention he and the team received. It's not often that amateurs just starting out are lauded for their accomplishments before having even gotten to the top. Being recognized by these climbers, whom he admired, affirmed for Tyrhee his decision to pursue his interest in outdoor recreation. There on the glacier at 14,200 feet, the only thing shining brighter than the blinding white snow was Tyrhee's dazzling smile as he hauled his pack and sled into camp. He had truly arrived.

The team enjoyed their welcome into the greater community of climbers. There was no pretense or posturing, as every person there had proven their qualifications for membership into this elite club simply by having made the journey. The price of admission was the long walk up from the Kahiltna Glacier. But what struck several members of the Expedition Denali team was the presence of several other African-American climbers who shared their passion for adventure and who had made the same trip by other means.

"So Advance Base Camp had way more flava than usual," Adina said. "We had a bunch of positive interactions and conversations about the aim of our project, diversity in the outdoors, and climbing culture in general. I wouldn't say there were necessarily moments of utter clarity or epiphany, but for me there were definitely moments that were important for me to process what we were doing and the context in which it was happening."

Scanning the camp and the snow-covered peaks beyond it, Adina couldn't help but smile at the fact that she found herself standing at 14,200 feet on the slopes of Denali. Though Adina's parents used to take her on countless trips into the mountains, she recalled those outings with mixed feelings. She remembers whining, as children do, through many long hikes plagued with mosquitos, chilly wet clothing, blisters, and sunburn. She told me later that her father David still chuckles at the memory of the little girl whom he once had to ply with candy and promises of special treats just to go on a hike—this same young woman who now sought out every wooded path and rocky trail—or snowy peak—she could find. Looking back, Adina's not quite sure when her attitude changed, but as an adult she fully appreciates the peace and quiet that come with getting out into nature.

As a graduate student at Purdue University in Indiana, she led friends on long weekend getaways in the Smoky Mountains, a subrange of the Appalachians along the border of Tennessee and North Carolina. Like a lot of students, she had little money, but Adina was pleased to discover that she could enjoy exercise and entertainment for the price of a full gas tank and a campsite permit. While tromping along the trails through the Smokies, she finally discovered a profound and abiding love for the outdoors, as a grown-up on her own terms.

One of Adina's greatest joys as an adult was going for what she called a scramble. With nothing more technical than a good pair of hiking shoes, she headed into most any mountain range and walked established trails or used a map and compass to navigate her way to the top of some high peak. Whether with friends or by herself, Adina liked to venture into the wild to escape the distraction of cell phones, computers, and the general noise of society. During these quiet times, she enjoyed the opportunity to become better acquainted with her hiking companions or be alone with her own thoughts, which was often wrestling with some complex engineering challenge.

By working past the physical discomfort she felt as a child while hiking with her father, she was able to experience the joy of alpine adventures across the most stunning landscapes of North America. Now, as a mentor in her Seattle community, Adina works to help young people appreciate the outdoors in much the same way her father planted the seed in her. Adina's goal as a member of the Expedition Denali team was to demonstrate to those kids and the world that even someone who wasn't particularly fond of hiking as a child could grow to love it and excel at it.

DURING THOSE FEW DAYS ON DENALI, THERE WERE PROBABLY MORE African-Americans at 14 Camp than ever before in the mountain's long history. Also in camp at that time, on a different expedition led by top American alpinist Conrad Anker, were veteran NOLS instructor Philip Henderson and professional snowboarder Ryan Hudson. These two Black men perhaps best represented the wide spectrum of African-Americans in the world of mountaineering today. Henderson had twenty years of experience as a guide and wilderness educator and had spent the previous season on Mount Everest with Anker. He'd also worked for several years as an instructor at the Khumbu Climbing School in Nepal, where he and several other volunteers helped train the Sherpas in mastering the technical skills and techniques of modern alpinism. In contrast, Ryan, a champion snowboarder who mentored minority youth who aspired to a life in outdoor recreation, was on Denali embarking on his first high-altitude mountaineering experience.

Despite having summited Mount Everest three times, Anker possessed the humility and congenial nature of a conscientious college professor. He was well acquainted with the Expedition Denali project, having met several of the climbers earlier that year at the Outdoor Retailer Winter Market in Salt Lake City. At 14 Camp he was graciously supportive of everyone there.

To celebrate the summer solstice, Anker hosted a party at 14 Camp. He had hauled along with his personal gear a sled equipped with an enormous expedition base camp tent and extra rations of specialty food, including cured meats and cheeses. He transformed the sled into a buffet table, laid out the fare he had brought, and then invited everyone to partake in the bounty. Anker, a consummate team leader, encouraged everyone to enjoy themselves after all the hard work they had endured getting to 14 Camp. His generous nature and sense of camaraderie raised the spirits not only of his own team, but of all around him.

Everyone gathered to pool the best treats from their own food supplies to make an assortment of appetizers. One climber prepared a concoction of dried blueberries, strawberries, and cranberries topped with butter, brown sugar, honey, granola, crushed walnuts, and oatmeal. After two weeks of climbing on the glacier, the sticky sweet morsels delivered a sense of warmth and nourishment that went well beyond the energy they provided. Gestures such as this forged a bond among all those present. The climbers laughed, chatted, and traded climbing stories as they nibbled on gourmet cheeses and salami. Someone managed to play a selection of music on an iPod through a pair of tinny portable speakers, and there was even dancing.

Expedition Denali team member Erica Wynn sat watching the revelry at this party held 14,200 feet above sea level with a sense of awe, finding herself a bit disoriented by the surprising sense of community and friendship. She was also nothing short of amazed that everyone had been able to summon so much enthusiasm and create such a festive atmosphere in this hostile environment. As they reveled in their shared adventure, Erica felt part of a greater whole.

It was the summer solstice of 2013, and the one hundredth anniversary of the first ascent of Denali. A photograph was taken of everyone gathered at Advance Base Camp. The occasion was inspiring and the image, depicting an unprecedented and incredibly broad mix of ages, ethnicities, nationalities, and genders, served as an inspiring symbol of climbing's future.

Looking at this photograph weeks later, after everyone was off the mountain, no one could ever again accept the claim that climbing is "something that Black folks just don't do."

Profile

Ryan Hudson

Ryan Hudson paced in small circles in the falling snow as he waited his turn to drop. The overcast sky of a sunless day mirrored his dark mood and sense of foreboding. His pulse thrummed in his temples. He clenched his fists against the involuntary spasms of the muscles in his forearms, which seemed to be rippling like waves over his back, down his legs, and all the way to his toes. He shook out his arms, trying to release the tension, uncertain whether the anxiety he felt was relieved or exacerbated by the cold. To say that he was nervous was an understatement. There at the top of the freestyle course of The North Face Masters of Snowboarding competition at Snowbird, Utah, Ryan was having trouble reconciling the reality of where he was now and where not so long ago he thought he would be at this moment in his life.

"What am I doing?" he asked himself. "I'm not supposed to be here. I'm way out of my league!"

The year was 2010, and Ryan found himself in the middle of what seemed to be a dream. Outfitted in the latest technical gear from The North Face, he was moments away from making his first run as a competitive snowboarder.

"Hudson! You're up! Get in the gate!" shouted a voice over the loadspeaker, startling Ryan out of his reverie. Determined to embrace reality, he lowered his goggles over his eyes, hoisted his board to one shoulder, and jogged over the packed snow to the starting line.

"Right away, the clouds broke, the sun came out, and I could see the entire run from top to bottom," Ryan said. "The moment just became this perfect, perfect moment. So I took a deep breath. Immediately my nervousness was gone. I felt really comfortable. And I dropped."

Ryan abandoned all his doubt and inhibitions and plummeted at an astounding speed toward the bottom of the run. Carving tight, graceful turns down the slope, he knew this was the culmination of a path he had begun designing for himself many years ago.

The youngest of five children, Ryan was raised by a single mother in San Diego. Homeless from the moment he was born, he had few clear prospects for a better future.

"Most of my childhood was immersed in this impoverished lifestyle," Ryan told me in an interview. "I grew up in and out of shelters. We were sleeping on the streets and pretty much did whatever we could to get by, but in the lowest form of living."

For as long as he could remember, Ryan had none of the basic advantages most people take for granted. He had no place to call home, no bed of his own to sleep in, not even regular meals. Though he went to school, he often faced the ridicule of his classmates for being homeless. He typically wore dirty and tattered clothing, and he was embarrassed by the free lunch he received, another indication of his status at the very bottom of American society. As many young people on assistance do, he often went hungry rather than endure the scorn of his fellow students for receiving a government handout.

But somehow, despite these circumstances, Ryan kept his grades up in school and a positive attitude. He dreamed of one day creating a better life for himself. At the age of fourteen, he took off on his own to make his way in the world.

"I did some research and found a shelter for teenagers and decided to move into this program called the Toussaint Academy," Ryan said. "It was a very well-kept program, but very strict in a lot of ways."

After so many years living on the streets of San Diego, Ryan was accustomed to being outside, riding his skateboard and playing with his friends. But the resident program at Toussaint kept him and the other young people under their care indoors. It might have been intended as a way to better monitor their behavior or a means of providing them with structure and keeping them safe. But for Ryan, the secure environment gave him the opportunity to look within himself and discover new talents.

"I started getting into a lot of things that really helped to flex my creativity and really brought out a part of me that I really didn't know was there," he said. "I got into music and got into writing. I got really into computers. And to this day, all those things are still a part of me."

Ryan found he had an aptitude for playing the drums, and through the rhythms he created on percussion instruments, he found focus and peace of mind while pounding out some of the pain and suffering he experienced as a child.

"A door opened up to opportunity, creativity, and positivity," Ryan said. "I closed myself off to everyone else, locked myself in the music room, and played the drums. I took that confidence and motivation that I found in playing the drums and put it toward writing, skateboarding, and the arts."

At the Toussaint Academy, Ryan found several worthwhile outlets for his many creative talents. And with the help of his instructors, he managed to get a good education in a supportive and intellectually stimulating environment. But Ryan still lacked a single focus toward which he could direct his emerging passions. That all changed the day he met

Chris Rutgers, founder of the Outdoor Outreach program, which provides disadvantaged young people positive experiences in nature. As part of the program, Rutgers led wilderness trips that took kids far out of their comfort zone in the city. Himself the product of a troubled childhood, Rutgers built Outdoor Outreach working out of his garage. Relying on used and donated equipment cobbled together on a ridiculously small budget, he created real-world opportunities for young people like Ryan to get outside and play. By providing them with a chance to see a world beyond the concrete, asphalt, and steel that makes up their urban existence, Outdoor Outreach offers them an alternative way of life to aspire to.

In 2004, Rutgers invited a few Toussaint kids with good grades and an interest in the outdoors to visit Big Bear, a mountain community about two hours from San Diego. Eager to experience something new—a cold climate—for the first time, Ryan signed up immediately. The other students slept during the bus ride, but he stared out the window, captivated by the sight of a landscape he'd never known. They arrived to see tall trees and snow-covered alpine slopes. For the first time, Ryan was able to see his own breath as it rose in wisps of steam like a puff of smoke.

"That was the first time I had experienced mountains. It was the first time I had seen or felt snow in my life aside from seeing it on TV," he said. "It was really an amazing moment, a real breathtaking moment for me being up in the mountains and getting a sense of knowing what different air smelled like and felt like in your lungs and experiencing so many new things all at once. It was a little overwhelming, but also very liberating."

Ryan tried snowboarding for the first time during that trip. Locking his boots into the bindings somehow felt natural, almost like he was made for them. The body positioning and movements reminded him of skateboarding, and after a few turns down the hill, he knew instinctively that this was the thing he had been looking for—the thing he could devote his life to and a way to find some happiness.

"I immediately fell in love," Ryan said. His eyes lit up as he recalled the moment. He loved the steep downhill runs. He loved linking turns together and the chill of the wind on his cheeks. Ice crystals stung the exposed skin on his face as he smiled with utter delight. "I had a really, really good first day," Ryan said.

Ryan returned to San Diego determined to somehow make it back to the mountains. Impressed by how quickly Ryan had taken to snowboarding, Rutgers invited him to work at Outdoor Outreach as a junior instructor. Though it didn't take him back to the mountains, Ryan spent that summer in San Diego learning a variety of different recreational activities, which he went on to share with other students in the program.

"When I first started, spring was just coming around, and I got into surfing for the first time. And even that came easily," Ryan said. "I didn't take up surfing avidly, but it was a similar experience for me, and I fell in love with being in the ocean."

Ryan had gone to the beach as a child, but like many children without adult supervision or guidance, he had never really learned to enjoy playing in the waves. In fact, he had seldom even gotten in the water.

"This was the first time I really interacted with the ocean and learned things about the ocean," Ryan said. "I learned about stingrays and currents and quality of water and different things about the ocean that a lot of kids don't get to experience. They're five miles away, but they don't ever get to see or experience it. That's just the way they live. That's the way I lived, and suddenly I had a chance to change all that."

By connecting with other young people who also came from impoverished backgrounds, Ryan discovered a powerful life's mission. Through

Outdoor Outreach, he would help inspire and empower underprivileged youth. By offering them transformational experiences in nature, he hoped to help them become productive and successful adults. In the process, Ryan had the opportunity to do many things, including rock climbing and mountain biking. He began to allow himself to imagine a life far from the poverty and the homeless shelters where he had grown up. Unfortunately when he graduated from high school, he had to leave the protective environment of the Toussaint Academy.

"When you're done, they pretty much kick you out," Ryan said. "I didn't know what to do."

A year later, with little to occupy his time or his mind, Ryan found himself floundering. With no gainful employment and no place to live, he found himself back on the streets again. "I spent too much time skateboarding and not enough time looking for a job or applying to college," he said. "I was in a place where I felt really low. And I didn't have any stable family members to turn to. I was sleeping on a friend's couch."

Looking for a solution, Ryan reconnected with Rutgers at Outdoor Outreach. He wanted to pursue his interest in snowboarding and perhaps make a life for himself working in outdoor recreation. He simply didn't know how to go about making it happen. Unfortunately, Outdoor Outreach could only offer him part-time work at best and no real opportunity to advance. In the hopes of encouraging Ryan to pursue a career path similar to his own, Rutgers suggested that he leave San Diego and go somewhere he could snowboard every day while working some menial job at night. With few better alternatives and nothing keeping him in California, Ryan took Rutgers's advice and moved to Salt Lake City.

"He bought me a plane ticket and gave me a hundred bucks cash," Ryan said. "He put me on the plane, and I've been here ever since."

Chris Rutgers's faith in him changed Ryan Hudson's life. He wasn't given a free pass or privileged access to unlimited opportunities and financial resources. But he got a chance to do better and the obligation to live up to the expectations of a mentor who believed in him. When as a society we struggle with how best to secure the future success of young people otherwise at risk of continuing in the cycle of poverty, sometimes the solution lies simply in providing them with a dream and encouraging them to make it come true.

Ryan got a job washing dishes at the Peruvian Lodge at Alta ski resort and moved into a small apartment that he shared with several roommates. He dedicated himself to becoming a better snowboarder.

"My schedule was simple," Ryan said. "I woke up in the morning. I ate breakfast. I snowboarded from 9:00 to 3:00, came home, and washed dishes from 4:00 to 11:00 and went to sleep. Rinse and repeat for six months."

Plowing all of his extra cash into snowboarding gear and discount lift tickets, he hit the slopes every day that winter. In the summer, he returned to San Diego to work for Rutgers at Outdoor Outreach. When he returned to Alta the following winter to continue his life as an amateur snowboarder, he found that his skills had improved enough to take it to the next level.

"I watched one of the big mountain snowboard competitions called The North Face Masters," Ryan said. "A lot of guys were out there. I felt like I could do some of the things those guys could do. And that kind of gave me the thought and the idea that I could do something like that."

As he matured as an athlete, he built relationships with the other boarders on the hill and within the ski community. Eventually he came to the attention of The North Face, which had recently put together an initiative called Outdoor Exploration and Community Development. Much like the Outdoor Outreach program in San Diego, it aimed to expose disadvantaged young people to activities like skiing and snowboarding. When they learned of Ryan's background and obvious talent, they offered him a chance to compete in The North Face Masters event.

"They paid for my registration, got me a spot in the comp, sent me a box of gear, full outerwear and everything," Ryan said. "It was amazing."

On the day of the competition, however, his nerves threatened to get the better of him. As luck would have it, he was the very last competitor on the roster—which gave him plenty of time to wrestle with feelings of self-doubt.

"It was really scary for me being there," Ryan said. "I didn't feel that I at all deserved to be there until it came time for me to drop. And then I had a really good day."

He negotiated the course with the same love and passion that he did every day and stayed firmly planted on his feet. The music playing over the loudspeakers compounded his excitement as he danced over the snow on his board. Carving a last high-speed turn past a throng of spectators, he pumped his arms into the air and the crowd erupted in a chorus of loud cheers.

"At the end of the day, I placed seventeenth out of ninety men and they gave me the Young Gun Award, which they give to the most up-and-coming rider twenty-five and under that they think is the future," Ryan said. "That for me was amazing. Just the feeling of hearing my name called, getting up and going on stage, and someone handing me an award. It was the first award that I had ever won. It was the first recognition I'd ever gotten for anything I had ever done in my life. It was really, really powerful. I definitely cried on stage."

Ryan Hudson's career as a professional snowboarder was launched that day. In a remarkable journey from the streets of San Diego to the slopes of Snowbird, he defied the odds to make a life for himself in the upper echelons of the adventure sports community. Today, Ryan not only works a day job at The North Face retail store in Salt Lake City, he also serves as a brand ambassador and member of the Snowbird snowboarding team. He travels around the country as a role model and mentor for at-risk youth.

Ryan is an inspiring example of what a person can accomplish when given a bit of support and encouragement to pursue their dreams. But what is especially compelling about his story is his willingness to put in the hard work necessary to make his ambitions a reality. Washing dishes was a worthwhile means to achieve his goals, and Ryan undoubtedly enjoys a much greater sense of satisfaction today for having made his way almost entirely on his own.

Three years after his professional debut at Snowbird, Ryan was on Denali at 14 Camp enjoying a celebration of the summer solstice. It was Ryan's impressive work ethic that brought him to the attention of The North Face climbing team leader and world-class mountaineer Conrad Anker. Working with several members of the company's brand ambassadors, Anker had put together a program to help expose young athletes to different kinds of adventure sports. In particular he wanted to give skiers and snowboarders like Ryan—who were accustomed to spending most of their time on the slopes at ski resorts—the opportunity to test their skills in a mountaineering environment. In 2011 Anker had led the program's first group of snowboarders to the summit of Denali. Two years later, he aimed to do it again, and this time he invited Ryan to come along. But the young man, just coming into his own as an athlete, initially felt the familiar tugs of doubt and uncertainty.

"I really felt like he asked the wrong person," Ryan said. "And it took me four months to say yes. When he asked me, I was terrified. I really didn't know what he was asking of me. I had never really heard of Denali before the project he did the previous winter. I told him I really couldn't say no. But given enough time, I finally said yes."

In addition to Ryan Hudson, Anker's small team of new climbers included his adopted son Max Lowe, who'd received a grant as a National Geographic Young Explorer, NOLS instructor Philip Henderson, ski mountaineers Brody Leven and Kasha Rigby, and pro snowboarders Jeremy Jones, Ralph Backstrom, and Jacqui Edgerly. Also along on the 2013 Denali trip was Anker's good friend, best-selling author and mountaineer Jon Krakauer.

Rather than spending the night at the landing strip, which is common on any ascent of Denali, Anker had rallied his team for a push to Camp I at 7,800 feet as soon as their planes touched down. Ryan learned on the fly, shouldering his heavy load and heading up the slope of the Kahiltna Glacier for the five-mile trek to Camp I. He had little opportunity to acclimate and just did his best to keep up. Upon arriving at his first camp on Denali, he was reeling.

"It was a solid twenty-five hours from the day we arrived in Anchorage. Twenty-five hours on the move and I was whopped," Ryan said. "I didn't know what I was doing. And all the while I'm completely unorganized, completely beside myself not knowing what I'm doing, what I'm getting into, how to do any of this. I'm just going with the flow."

The following morning, Anker led his team up to the second campsite at 11,000 feet. That push was the most difficult part of the journey for Ryan.

"I didn't eat well that morning. I didn't have a good breakfast, and I wasn't really fueling during the move," he said. "And so by the time I got to Camp II I was exhausted. I could say that was my worst day physically."

As Ryan moved his gear laboriously up the mountain, he questioned his ability to operate so far out of his comfort zone.

"Mentally the entire trip was pretty bad for me, just battling all the emotions and so many feelings," he said. "But I still tried to keep a cool head and stay focused and not make any mistakes. It was really emotionally taxing."

But he managed to keep pace with the rest of the team. He successfully negotiated the rockfall danger at Windy Corner and made it safely to Advance Base Camp at 14,200 feet. At last given an opportunity to rest and collect himself, Ryan was able to fully grasp where he was. In the tent city and later during the solstice party thrown by Anker, Ryan finally put his doubts and misgivings behind him and embraced the experience of being on Denali.

"That for me was the moment in which I felt this is it. This is real. This is what we're here for," Ryan said. "This is why Conrad is in love with it and why all these guys fell in love with it, and I'm just now seeing it for the first time. And slowly I'm falling in love with it too."

CHAPTER SIX

14 Camp

A HALO OF BAD WEATHER KEPT THE EXPEDITION DENALI CLIMBERS socked in at 14 Camp for five days and put them behind schedule. Stuck in a holding pattern, the team eagerly awaited a break in the weather. When at last a small window of opportunity presented itself on June 25, the team decided to take advantage of it and depart the following day. Blowing snow and low-hanging clouds could still be seen gusting violently around the peak from camp, but the winds had died down just enough for the team to make their next ascent to High Camp at 17,200 feet possible.

Their goals were ambitious. They intended to climb past the cache they had deposited a few days earlier at 16,000 feet and use a set of fixed ropes to ascend a near-vertical 1,000-foot wall of ice with fully loaded packs. At this stage they had to leave their sleds behind, for this was arguably the most technical part of the entire route and there was no good way to pull them up the ice wall.

The National Park Service installs the fixed ropes each year to ensure safe passage for the climbers. Two ropes, one designated for the ascent and the other for the descent, offer a secure and relatively speedy method of reaching High Camp. But as these ropes are shared, the route is restricted to a single-file line, and there is no way to pass others ahead on the rope. Traffic on the mountain is reduced to the speed of the slowest climber, and this section is often plagued with congestion.

The next day, despite falling snow and the unseasonably warm temperatures that had them worried again about rockfall, the I-Team decided to go for it all the same. Even when the sun barely sets, an alpine start comes early; unfortunately Expedition Denali had some difficulty breaking camp in a timely fashion. When members of the I-Team made their way from tent to tent at 5:00 A.M. to announce that it was time to go, they found it difficult to rouse the team. Getting nineteen tired souls motivated for a major push over steep terrain during a whiteout under the threat of an avalanche was far more challenging than they had anticipated. Rosemary, in particular, was exhausted and suffering from nasal congestion and a mild, but increasingly painful, headache that was likely the result of the altitude. Yet when Aaron shook the fabric of her tent, she rallied her remaining energy, put on her boots, and fastened the buckles of her harness.

After melting a large quantity of snow for drinking water—they had learned their lesson—the team prepared for a mass exodus. With no sleds to balance their loads, everyone's pack was heavier than it had been at any other point on the expedition. As Rosemary hoisted her burden first to her knee, then to her shoulder, and finally to her back, the weight pressed down heavily on her spirit.

"The trek would have been difficult even if we'd had ample time, but unfortunately because we were behind, we were creeping closer to the risk of rockfall, so we were in kind of a hurry," she said.

Shobe pulled the straps of his pack to draw the load tight to his back and cinched his hip belt one last notch to settle as much of the weight as he could squarely on his hips. Struggling against both the strain of the early morning and less sleep than he might have liked, he resigned himself to the task at hand. With his ice ax dangling from a leash on his wrist, he walked over to inspect the knots tied to the harnesses of each member of his rope team.

There was just one last thing to do before the team could get under way. Shobe approached Billy, who spread his arms to reveal the intricate array of climbing hardware and nylon webbing he'd put in place. With the ease of long practice, Billy recited and confirmed each of the critical steps he had taken to assure not only his safety but that of each member of his rope team.

"Harness strapped high and tight, leg loops in place, the buckle doubled back for safety, check!" Billy said as he confirmed each item with a tug of his gloved hands. "A properly dressed figure-8 knot tied and clipped to both strong points of the harness with a locking carabiner, check! Two cordelettes tied to the rope with prusik knots clipped to a second locking carabiner, check! And a pack leash clipped to the rope and girth-hitched to the pack's haul loop, check!"

In the event of a fall, this setup was what would keep him alive. The ritual of checking systems had forged a solid bond between him and the others who shared his rope. Inspecting one another's gear was an unspoken promise to have each other's back and put their own lives on the line to protect a teammate in trouble. Shobe patted Billy on the shoulder, careful not to topple his balance as he teetered under the massive load. Next he checked Adina.

By the time the team finally set off, they were dangerously behind schedule, and it was crucial that they make good time now. If the team reached the fixed lines during the heat of the day, when the ice and snow began to melt, they would in all likelihood encounter rockfall and put everyone in grave danger. Shobe had found the climb to the fixed lines quite thrilling when they'd gone up to bury their cache a few days before, but all that changed under the full weight of their gear.

"It was pretty exciting at first, but this was no cakewalk," Shobe said. "In my mind, I'm thinking I've got to climb this route just one more time and it's done. The next time I see it I'm going to be happy because then I'm on my way home."

Under the added weight of their packs, a few people were having difficulty negotiating the icy path. Rosemary struggled to keep up with her rope team. With tears of anguish and frustration streaming down her cheeks and stinging her skin in the chill wind, she leaned into her straps and continued to take another step and then another. The going was slow, but she never stopped.

The seconds seemed to tick by faster and faster as the sun rose—along with the temperature. As melting ice loosened its precarious hold on tons of rock, stones the size of a man's fist began tumbling across the path in front of them. Though the fixed lines were almost within reach, Aaron and the other instructors made the tough call that the entire team turn around to retreat back to 14 Camp.

More ashamed than relieved, Rosemary stood in her tracks, feeling the weight of responsibility for their slow pace settle on her shoulders. Though she was grateful for the chance to rest, she blamed herself for reducing the team's forward movement to a crawl. For the first time, Expedition Denali had made negative progress. The strain of the return trip was made worse by the fact that everyone was struggling with disappointment.

"That just bust my bubble because I did not want to climb that son-of-a-bitch all over again. So we had to turn around and go back," Shobe said. "But that's the way it goes. We had to make a call, and coming back down was the smart thing to do."

Usually one of the most energetic and upbeat members of the team, Rosemary walked along the path with her head downcast and her heart sorrowful. As they arrived back at 14 Camp, she immediately got busy pitching her tent, fortifying wind walls, melting snow, and preparing dinner. These shared tasks comforted her, and despite herself, she couldn't help smiling.

Though Rosemary held herself responsible for having to turn back, no one on the team blamed her. They were all beaten down, exhausted, and discouraged, but they each did their utmost to lift one another's spirits.

"I am not a fast hiker. That combined with the crazy heavy packs and the fact that I wasn't feeling all too well that morning made it a tough day," Rosemary said. "But no matter what, I always knew that everyone had my back and that nobody was judging me or grudging against me. It was awesome to be surrounded by such a supportive and understanding group of people."

That night everyone turned in early to get some much-needed sleep. And despite crushing fatigue, they braced themselves for an even earlier departure the following day. This time, they were up by 2:00 A.M. and set off at a brisk pace, determined to improve upon their performance of the day before. Still under the weight of their monstrously heavy packs, the team charged forward with every ounce of strength they possessed. But the going was tough. As she walked carefully along the route, Erica looked down to see that one of her crampons had slipped from the toe of her boot. Grinding her teeth in exasperation, she cursed to herself as she bent down to fix it. Her fingers numb with cold, she fumbled with the straps and buckles and finally managed to get it back in place with I-Team's Madhu Chikkaraju's assistance. But in the moments it took to do so, they blocked the long line of climbers behind them, creating a traffic jam.

Embarrassed to be the cause of the delay, Erica moved as quickly as she could to keep pace with her rope team after that. She took comfort in the fact that no one nagged at her to hurry. It seemed that the climbers understood that it could just as easily have been any one of them to lose a crampon and bitching about it wouldn't do any good.

Although they enjoyed relatively clear skies and significantly less wind, the climbers still suffered from the effects of altitude, gravity, heat, and the steep upward climb. The combination of direct sunshine and the physical intensity of the climb caused everyone to overheat, even as the snow on the mountain and the ambient temperature of the air left them chilled.

"Depending on my level of exertion, I either felt like I was freezing or burning up," Adina said. "And I had a hard time anticipating my needs and finding the right layers."

Eventually, the team arrived at the base of the headwall. There, the route became a near vertical climb up 1,000 feet of ice. Even with the help of fixed lines, they all knew this was the single most difficult feature on the entire climb. And though the ropes were there to help them, the climbers could only go as fast as the person in front of them. Several members of the team were concerned about the pressure of having a buildup of impatient climbers behind them.

"Once again, I felt pressured because we were creating a bottleneck on the fixed lines and I knew I had to keep going, but physically I was struggling," Adina said. It was nerve-racking enough to be worried about the risk of rockfall and still push herself as hard as she could. The prospect of having climbers right on her heels only exacerbated an already difficult challenge. Exhausted, she had to stop.

Looking behind him, Shobe saw Adina leaning heavily on the blade of her ice ax, which she'd planted solidly into the snow between the toes of her boots. She was resting her helmeted head against the ice wall in a state of almost total exhaustion. It was humbling for Shobe to see the team's strongest climber so thoroughly spent. The climb was tearing away at every fiber of their collective being, and yet they still had so far to go.

But Adina possessed the presence of mind to know when she'd had enough. She signaled to her rope team to stop. Removing her pack, she eased it down far enough to secure it to the closest snow anchor that held the fixed lines in place. A guide from another group on the way up behind her volunteered to carry her load the last remaining feet to the top of the headwall. Accepting help on this especially difficult part of the climb gave Adina the opportunity to rest, and in a few minutes she was able to recover enough strength to ascend with the others to a flat expanse within reach of their day's objective.

Once she made it to the top of the ridge, Adina and the other climbers were able to take a proper break, reconfigure their layering systems, refuel, and rehydrate. Even as they strapped their packs back on and started walking again, they felt a surge of pride at their progress. They had gotten through the biggest challenge of the day—maybe even of the entire expedition—and the rest of the way to their camp at 17,200 feet was relatively easy. Though they were tired from the long climb, their spirits were high.

"Nobody gave up," said Shobe. "Despite hitting the wall, crampons coming off, rockfalls, and all these things that we had to deal with, everybody was there. We weren't all at 100 percent all the time, but nobody ever gave up."

AS THEY MADE THEIR WAY TOWARD HIGH CAMP ALONG A NARROW ridge at the top of the West Buttress, the team was rewarded for their efforts with a spectacular view of the entire Alaska Range. Under a clear sky, the clouds beneath them looked like a vast white ocean, and the peaks of nearby mountains rose up from the depths like a chain of islands.

After making their way past a rocky outcropping called Washburns Thumb, they wearily trudged into their highest campsite at 17,200 feet. Though High Camp looked much like all the sites they had previously occupied, Adina explained that it felt different. "At 14 Camp you could hang out and talk to people. It was a lot more relaxed. High Camp was all business. I can't remember a minute there when we weren't doing something."

The climbers felt like the whole world lay beneath them. From where they stood, they could see most of their route, starting from the Kahiltna Glacier where the expedition began on the landing strip at 7,200 feet. A wide snowfield just below the mountain's peak, High Camp was the perfect final staging ground for a push to the top. Unfortunately though, several other parties had already taken up residence in the best campsites, and space was at a premium.

In most of the lower camps, Expedition Denali climbers had been able to take over a spot abandoned by a departing group. With minimal effort they had been able to fortify the walls of ice used by the last party to protect themselves against the wind, and they had been able to put up their tents in spots already flattened by others. But at High Camp, it required a great deal of effort to make each tent platform habitable. Several other teams, including Conrad Anker's, had been stuck at 14 Camp. As the weather had improved, there was a rush to make it to the summit before the window of opportunity closed.

But as the team set up their tents and hunkered down for the night, the weather rolled in on top of them. Driving snow and pounding winds began scouring their camp. The team worked furiously to build new walls of ice and snow around their nylon homes for protection. Battling the cold and low oxygen levels, the team struggled to hold their position. After they finally put the last block of ice into place, everyone retreated to their tents to wait out the storm.

Unfortunately "cooking" at High Camp was restricted to melting snow for drinking water. At higher altitudes, turning ice into water requires considerably more time and energy—and more of both to bring that water to a boil. So they subsisted on rations of energy bars, candy, potato chips, nuts, dried fruit, and beef jerky.

Though the team had originally planned to head for the summit the next morning, the high winds and falling snow persisted and kept them pinned down through the following day. They spent the time resting in their tents or venturing outside to pack more snow onto the wind walls. Though a part of them was eager to continue on, they were equally content to rest and chat quietly in their tents.

Profile

Kai Lightner

As the Expedition Denali team members huddled in their tents at 17,200 feet, each likely wondered if everything that they had endured to get this far would be worth it. At that point, hardly any of the young people they hoped to inspire had any idea what these climbers were doing less than a vertical mile from the highest peak in North America. However, one young man was following their progress with great interest.

Tall for his age and thin, Kai Lightner was a middle schooler who loves to climb and takes full advantage of every opportunity to do so. But his dedicated coach, Emily Taylor, was an eight-hour drive away from Kai's home in North Carolina, and Kai received hands-on training with her only once a month. In between, his mother, Connie Lightner, a professor of mathematics at Fayetteville State University and a single mom, ran her son through the drills prescribed by Taylor and shuttled him once a week after school to a small gym with a twenty-five-foot climbing wall seventy-five miles from their home.

Kai had few peers to train with regularly and the only consistent male role model in his life was another coach, Shane Messer, who lived hundreds of miles away in Boston. Though Kai's race theoretically shouldn't have blocked his progress, the reality was that it was a daunting task for a teenage boy to carry the burden of being the first African-American to potentially be the best competition sport climber in the world. But that was his goal.

Kai Lightner was brought to my attention in the lead up to Expedition Denali. Videos of him climbing were circulating around the internet on YouTube, and it didn't take long for me to track him down. As it happened, I was acquainted with a few colleagues in the Southeast who were supporting his efforts to realize his dream. To introduce myself as a journalist, after first contacting his mother, I struck up a friendship with Kai via Facebook and a few phone calls. He was the feature of a profile story I wrote that was published in *Rock & Ice* magazine.

Kai was excited to learn about Expedition Denali and a team of Black climbers who shared his ambitions to reach great heights.

"As a competitive climber, I know the indescribable feeling of breaking new ground. When I watch others fight hard to reach a rarely (or never) achieved goal, it's almost like I can feel the incredible excitement that's rushing through them," Kai wrote me. "I checked back on your blog each day to track their progress. It was exciting! I hope other minorities will come to realize the amazing adventures that one can experience outdoors and spread the trend throughout our community."

For one so young, Kai seemed to have an adult's understanding of the sheer audacity of his own aspirations. But as a young man who aimed for world-class competition, he wanted his skill and talent to speak for themselves—he wanted to be known not as a Black climber but as a great climber. With his coach Taylor's help, Kai was getting a good education in what it took to be an outstanding athlete. Taylor is a fierce Black woman with the drive and determination to overcome any obstacle. Working with Kai, she blended maternal protective instincts with a tough-love attitude meant to push her young charge to live up to the demands of his ambitions.

One of the first African-American women to successfully summit Yosemite's El Capitan, Taylor is an accomplished climber herself.

The owner of her own coaching business, she has guided hundreds of young people through the rigors of competition. But she was especially supportive of Kai, both because he was so talented and because she feared that he might be overlooked or even ignored by the broader community of climbers who were likely unaccustomed to seeing such a high-achieving Black kid.

Kai started climbing when he was only seven years old. During a visit to a rock gym in Boston, he was given the chance along with several other kids in a group of first-time visitors to ascend a route rated 5.9. Challenging even for an experienced climber, the route got the best of Kai, and he was beside himself with frustration when he was unable to make it to the top.

"It completely shut me down. I was in tears, crying with snot running down my nose," Kai remembered. "I was really upset and they made me leave. But I kept coming back trying to climb that climb. And when I did, I wanted to climb everything else."

No one knew it at the time, but Kai was later diagnosed with attention-deficit/hyperactivity disorder (ADHD). Unable to concentrate or even sit still for very long, he was impossible to control and frequently erupted in temper tantrums and fits of hysterical crying.

"But all that really changed when we discovered climbing," his mother Connie said. "He wanted to do it so badly, somehow in his mind he was able to pull it together and make it happen."

Once Kai had successfully climbed that 5.9, his innate talent started to reveal itself. Faced with the emotionally neutral and physically unapologetic nature of rock climbing—a sport that would not tolerate his erratic behavior—he managed to overcome those mood swings. When she realized what a positive effect climbing had on her son, Connie Lightner did everything she could to support him in the pursuit of his dreams. Despite her busy schedule as an academic, she went well beyond her own comfort zone to create climbing opportunities for him. She frequently drove him long distances so that Kai could train in prominent outdoor sport-climbing areas like the Red River Gorge in Kentucky and the New River Gorge in West Virginia.

"The fact that my mother let me go back to the Red and the New meant a lot because my mother doesn't like anything to do with nature or bugs or rocks or trees or anything," Kai said. "But I love the rock formations. And when I get to the top of the wall and I look out at nature, I love how beautiful it is. I also like climbing on rock because it's a completely different feeling of achievement."

"He has the ambition to always go back for it, to reach the top. He never gives up," Taylor said. "Other kids his age, of the four hundred or so I've coached, are seldom so self-motivated. Only one kid has ever said, 'I want to be the best in the world.' And that's Kai."

A combination of natural ability, desire, and patience all influence Kai's prowess on rock walls. He seems infinitely comfortable holding the most precarious positions. Even on steep overhangs, he takes his time, moving slowly from one solid hold to the next.

"He's a bionic sloth!" Taylor said. "He's the slowest moving climber you've ever seen. He'll just hang there and won't move until he's got it figured out."

His YouTube videos are agonizingly slow to watch as he makes his way up the most difficult routes. Yet when faced with a particularly hard section, seldom does Kai seem to get frustrated like most climbers. With incredible patience and persistence, he just works the problem out.

"I really think that's a sign of his character," Taylor said. "He probably gets that from his mother. He pushes himself the way she pushes him to do the best he can every time. It's his character that gets him to the top."

As of 2013, Kai held four consecutive titles in the Sport Climbing Series National Championships, which are held each year at Taylor's training gym, Stone Summit, in Atlanta. His victory in 2013 made him eligible for the International Federation of Sport Climbing Youth World Championships in Victoria, British Columbia. When he finished fourth in his first international competition, the sponsorship offers started rolling in. He was immediately picked up as a team athlete working with major brands such as Evolv Sports & Designs and Salewa Mountain Sports Products. But Kai's mother won't let all this success go to his head.

"He knows that climbing is always contingent on keeping his grades up in school," Connie said. "He's a straight-A student."

Although he hasn't picked a career path just yet, Kai has already recognized his potential role in helping to encourage his peers and next generations to take up the sport of rock climbing. He is well aware that his mere presence at major events—as well as his talent for ascending difficult routes—goes a long way toward creating positive role models for others.

"Race doesn't change your ability to climb," Kai said. "Don't get me wrong. I am a very proud African-American climber. I believe that if African-Americans were exposed to the sport, more people would be into it. I hope that more African-American kids see me and know that it's possible."

After his years of hard work and discipline, Kai has earned the respect of his coaches, teammates, fellow competitors, and a growing number of journalists like me. Smart, articulate, and polite, he epitomizes the very best that an American youth and world-class athlete has to offer. Unfortunately these are character traits that many outside of the climbing community may fail to see.

In the late fall of 2012, while traveling through Washington, DC, on one of many weekend road trips to train at a climbing gym far from home, Kai and his mom Connie stopped at a gas station to refuel the car and use the restroom. On the way out of the facilities, an attendant pulled up Kai's shirt, frisked him, and accused him of stealing, with no evidence of wrongdoing. Released, he ran back to his car, reduced to tears. That incident, coming just after the national case of the unjust acquittal of George Zimmerman in the case of Trayvon Martin in Florida in 2013, scared and angered Connie, who wants people to see her son as the mild-mannered, straight-A, national sport-climbing champion that he is.

Although the state of our country saddened her, Connie took comfort in the fact that Kai has always been supported and encouraged in his climbing career. "I am fortunate that my son is surrounded by a rock climbing community that has never seen race," Connie said. "Despite it being a predominantly white sport, he has never felt different or outcast despite the fact that he is usually the only Black person at events. My fear is that outside of this community, his reality is very different."

That's likely true for most African-American youth, and I can't help but wonder how many more might benefit from the same sense of safety and support offered by the climbing community.

In their tents at 17,200 feet, as the Expedition Denali team prepared to make their final push for the summit, they could take comfort in the knowledge that their efforts may make a difference in the lives of more young people like Kai.

CHAPTER SEVEN

To the Summit

JUNE 26 WAS EXPEDITION DENALI'S NINETEENTH DAY ON THE MOUNTAIN. After one full day spent cocooned in their tents, Aaron Divine rolled out of his sleeping bag in the dim but persistent light of the Alaskan dawn and saw that the weather had cleared. A radio check of the barometric pressure, wind direction, and wind speed confirmed what he could see out the front flap of his tent at 6:00 A.M.: It was time to move.

The long wait at Advance Base Camp had created a backlog of climbers at High Camp waiting to push for the summit, and as he went around rousing the team, Aaron counted more than sixty climbers preparing to head up the mountain that day. The four-mile climb from 17,200 would involve 3,120 feet of elevation gain and a long walk across one of the deadliest parts of the mountain.

"That from the get-go made me a little bit trepidatious about being in that mix," he said. "I think it worked out well that other groups were also aware of our size and they purposely went before us so that everybody had some space."

Among the climbers heading for the summit that morning were members of Conrad Anker's team of The North Face athletes. Unlike the others, though, they hadn't spent the night at High Camp but made for the summit in a single push all the way from Advance Base Camp at 14,200 feet. Ryan Hudson said later, "That day was both the most terrifying and the most magnificent day of the whole trip."

As Anker's team made their way up the headwall, past the fixed ropes and toward Denali Pass, Ryan began to realize that he, along with writer Jon Krakauer, was well out in front of everyone else.

"We were just keeping a more efficient pace," Ryan said. "I followed step for step. We kind of got into this groove where we just pulled away. Along the trail, he's coaching me and giving me tips and really teaching me about the mountain."

When Anker's team stopped to rest at High Camp, they ran into Expedition Denali and the other teams preparing to head for the summit. Though they all spread out over the route along a span of two or three miles, the mountain nonetheless seemed crowded in places. At certain narrow sections where the climbers could pass through only one at a time, there were bottlenecks. "The Autobahn being one of them," Aaron said, "where travel only goes as fast as the slowest rope team."

A narrow trail situated along a steep slope, the Autobahn is the most direct route from High Camp to Denali Pass. With conditions that can range from sheer ice to deep snow with severe avalanche danger, more fatalities have occurred here than anywhere else on the mountain. Though that made everyone a bit nervous, the blue skies overhead filled them with optimism. "We're going to make it!" Rosemary thought to herself.

Even as a mass of cloud cover swept over the mountain when they were less than a mile out from High Camp, no one doubted that they would be successful in their bid to reach the summit. As they ascended the steep slope of the Autobahn, the wind picked up speed and snow began to fall. But with lighter packs, the climbers enjoyed the relative ease of scaling the mountain burdened only by water and a few ounces of food. Though the wind began howling all around them with growing intensity, everyone leaned into the mountain and continued carefully planting one foot after the other. Now almost two miles from their tents, they eventually made it safely to Denali Pass at 18,200 feet.

"Me and the other instructors were kind of watching the weather pretty closely, intently, seeing spots of blue sky, or sucker holes as folks will often call them," Aaron said. "It appeared that we might be able to pop above the immediate cloud layer and climb into better weather."

The weather did indeed get much better. Looking out from the top of Denali Pass, Rosemary was encouraged by several patches of blue amid the gray skies overhead—everyone was. But as they continued to climb, the effects of the higher altitude began to weigh them down. Erica experienced not only profound exhaustion but a burning sensation in her lungs. Yet up ahead she could see the summit—and it was so close. "It's right there," she thought to herself.

Meanwhile, farther up the mountain, Ryan Hudson and Krakauer kept climbing at a brisk pace. Although they weren't roped together, they had formed a bond. They came from vastly different backgrounds, but they had found a sort of kinship in the mountains, and Krakauer was teaching Ryan what he could from his long years of experience exploring the world's rocky peaks.

"Mind you, I didn't know who Jon Krakauer was before this trip," Ryan said. "But it meant a lot to me to get to know him rather than coming in with prior knowledge of all his writings and everything that he had accomplished in mountaineering. To me, he was just Jon."

As they made their way toward the summit, they shared stories and cracked jokes like old buddies. Though he didn't realize it at the time,

Ryan was having his anxieties put to rest by a master storyteller, and thus distracted, he made short work of the grueling uphill grind toward the peak. At the very base of the summit ridge, with just 300 vertical feet to go, they stopped for a rest. They took off their packs, ate some food, drank some water, and took in the amazing view.

"From that spot it was one of the most spectacular views I have ever seen, and Jon felt the same way," Ryan said. "We sat there and shared this amazing moment together, and Jon looked at me and said, 'You know what, Hudson? This has been the most amazing experience, and I am honored to be up here with you.'"

In that moment all the anxiety and doubt that Ryan had felt throughout his career as an athlete fell away. His skills and talents had just been acknowledged in a way that he had never experienced before, and in the months that followed, Ryan would look back on this moment and find it to be one of the most rewarding of his life. Tested against the elements, he had performed well despite his lack of advanced training or years spent in the mountains. It was then that Ryan decided to make big mountain snowboarding part of his career as a professional athlete.

"I'm not at the point where I can afford to go out into unknown ranges and start naming peaks after my kids," Ryan said. "But you know, man, it's all about falling in love with what you want to do, something that makes you feel good, something that you feel passionate about. Whether or not the color of my skin is black, pink, purple, orange, or green, we're all in it for the same thing."

While Ryan reveled in the moment, he suddenly became aware of a change in Krakauer's demeanor. Reaching down for his pack, Krakauer looked at him urgently.

"This is amazing and all," Krakauer told Ryan. "But we have to get the hell out of here. Something's coming and it's big and we're in the wrong place."

The sky was blue and the air was still. Ryan was terribly confused. But Krakauer's dire warning had left no room for argument. They immediately put on their packs and started heading down the mountain as fast as they could.

"There were still other teams on their way up," Ryan said. "And they were looking at us like we're crazy."

As they passed group after group, Krakauer spread the word that there was a major storm coming. With so many international teams on the mountain, not everyone understood what he was trying to convey, and many groups kept moving up. But then the sky suddenly turned dark and there was a horrifying clap of thunder.

THE I-TEAM HAD MADE THE DECISION TO PUSH ON FROM DENALI PASS, prepared to turn around at any moment if the weather didn't improve. But within fifteen minutes of leaving the pass, as they climbed up through a feature called Zebra Rocks, the snow began to slow, the wind died down, and the air around them grew still. Everyone's spirits rose as they climbed on through to Farthing Horn on the eastern edge of the Traleika Glacier. The team was elated to see the summit ridge clearly within view—though less excited to see the long line of climbers snaking their way up to the peak. They walked along the harrowing snow-and-ice-covered knife-edged spine of the mountain, all too aware of the devastating drop straight down on either side. After they'd made it past the Archdeacons Tower—a pyramid rock formation at just over 19,000 feet and well within full view of the summit—the trail opened onto an expansive plateau so broad and flat it was commonly known as the Football Field. The team took the opportunity to stop and rest there.

"Groups usually take a moment to catch their breath and reenergize," Aaron said of the Football Field. "And for us, as instructors and participants alike, we also take that moment to reassess what's happening. There were a number of folks on the peak trying to summit at that point. I was checking in with the other instructor team members, and we were talking about the congestion. And before finishing that conversation, we got the thunder."

All conversation ceased and every head turned at once toward the sound. They watched as a column of dark clouds came rolling in from the west. Then all at once, thunder began booming from every direction like cannon fire. Looking up, they saw climbers who had been heading toward the summit now barreling down the mountain at a breakneck pace. It was time to get out of there—and fast.

Still resting with their packs beside them on the snow, the Expedition Denali team was anxious but unsure what to do next. The summit was right there. Their goal was in sight and within reach, but everyone around them was suddenly in a mad scramble to head in the opposite direction. Despite the obvious danger of lightning strikes and now fresh flurries of snow, it still wasn't clear to everyone on the team that their next course of action was a full unconditional retreat.

But before confusion could turn to panic, Aaron took control of the situation. In a brilliant gesture of leadership, he turned to the group and spread his arms wide with his back to the mountain and the storm. He smiled broadly and declared loudly over the sound of the thunder: "Everybody, we're at 19,620 feet. Congratulations and welcome to your high point! It's time to start heading down."

The team stood there blinking in disbelief, but the urgency of their situation became shockingly clear as another clap of thunder echoed across the mountain. Startled into action, they grabbed their packs, hoisted them onto their shoulders, snapped on their hip belts, checked their knots, and began hustling back the way they had come. In the time it took for them to rally, the sky had completely covered over with clouds, and the snow, driven horizontal by the howling wind, blew directly in their faces. Within minutes, they were enveloped in a near total whiteout. Bright flashes of lightning struck continuously, followed by an instantaneous report of thunder, and everyone's metal gear became electrified. Holding her ice ax close to her ear, Erica was astonished to discover that she could actually hear it hum.

Having ascended the mountain at the end of the last rope team, Robby suddenly found himself at the front of the line. When word came down the string of climbers from Aaron—"Okay Robby, lead us out of here"—Robby found himself thrust into position as leader of the expedition.

But given the low visibility that was getting worse by the minute, Robby soon lost track of the visual markers—flags that had been set to mark their trail on the way up—and suddenly he couldn't see where he was going at all. Groping, unable to see through the whiteout, he couldn't effectively navigate his way forward.

"And then I started to feel this buzzing. The rope was running on my right side and my whole right arm and shoulder were vibrating and I was like, this isn't good. This isn't good!"

The air all around them was charged with electricity. As he led the group through a thundercloud—considering the very real possibility of being struck by lightning—Robby turned to Erica, the next climber in his rope team and said, "I don't like this."

Virtually blind, Robby stopped. Standing in the swirling wind, he was unsure what to do next. When he said as much out loud, Erica was immediately alarmed.

"What do you mean you don't know what to do?" she screamed. "You're an instructor!"

Keeping his panic in check, Robby pulled it together and yelled to Erica to call for Aaron. The electricity was literally humming through every piece of equipment and clothing on his body, and under the hood of his jacket, the static charge buzzed like a swarm of bees. As tiny sparks crackled around his head and down his arms, Robby recalled what he'd heard about a wet rope being like a steel cable. In his fear, he imagined it would conduct an electric current from one climber to the next should anyone be struck by lightning.

"I had carabiners, crampons and all this metal," Robby said. "And I thought all I want to do right now is untie, throw all this metal off, and stand on top of my pad."

Hearing Erica's call, Aaron raced down to where Robby stood. Aaron had recorded a set of waypoints with a GPS device on the way up the mountain, so he was better able to navigate without the benefit of visual markers. He got the team moving again.

Adina felt like she was running on pure adrenaline. She knew they needed to get down quickly before the snowfall became more serious or they got stuck behind other groups. And they still had a huge avalanche slope ahead of them.

Sure enough, there was a major traffic jam ahead on the Autobahn as another team stopped to assist a climber with acute altitude sickness. With so much activity along this narrow passage, it was difficult to maintain solid footing on the steep descent. A slab of ice and snow set at an obscenely acute angle, the Autobahn is challenging under even favorable circumstances. As she made her way across the slope, Erica leaned down to clip her harness into a loop of nylon webbing attached to a snow picket meant to protect her and the others in the event of a sudden stumble. Standing up, she took a step back and lost her balance. As she slipped, her ice ax fell out of her hand. Trying to arrest her descent with her knees, she yelled in a panic, "Falling!"

Robby, Scott, and DeBerry fell to the snow as one, their ice axes up, and locked themselves into a self-arrest position. Before Erica could fall even a few feet, her teammates caught her. As the rope pulled her harness tight, she managed to sink one of her crampons into the ice, then the other. Grabbing her ice ax where it hung from her wrist by a leash, she regained her balance, badly shaken but ready to keep moving. They still had a long way to go.

Once off the crowded Autobahn, the team continued to struggle through the foul weather, using GPS waypoints to follow a reverse course back to camp. The going gradually became easier and gravity worked in their favor. It took less than an hour to walk the remaining distance to the comfort and safety of their tents. But their window of opportunity was now closed, slammed violently shut by a freak electrical storm that climbers of Denali will likely talk about for years to come.

Once back at camp, after stowing their gear and removing their ropes, the members of the team made themselves as comfortable as possible. They boiled water for hot drinks and gobbled down handfuls of trail mix, candy, potato chips, and beef jerky. Though they were now out of immediate danger, adrenaline still coursed through their veins. And in spite of their fatigue, each tent group spoke excitedly about their harrowing descent.

The hurried trip down from the summit ridge had been terrifying for everyone. But since they had all made it safely back to High Camp, they could now look back on the events and laugh, marveling at the fact that they survived. They were very fortunate that things had not become any worse. Had they decided that achieving the summit was more important than their physical safety, they could easily have gotten stuck or jeopardized the safety of other groups. By taking the more sensible course of action and retreating, they would all live to climb another day. Though the summit had been so clearly within their reach, there was no question that turning around had been the right thing to do.

"When we finally made it back to camp, I felt amazing," Adina said. "Our team did a fantastic job, nature decided it was not our day, and we were all safe and had an incredible story."

That sense of satisfaction was shared by most everyone on the team—after such an intense experience they were all glad to be alive—but a few couldn't help but be a bit disappointed. "I'm glad we made it back safe and sound, but it's hard not to think about what might have been, that feeling of achievement if we had made it to the top," Erica had said. "I'm pretty goal oriented, so I consider success achieving what you set out to do."

But one of the hard realities of mountaineering is that not all expeditions result in a successful bid for the summit. You can have all the preparation, training, experience, expertise, and dumb luck in the world, but even the most elite alpinists are forced to turn around under certain circumstances. It's important to realize that mountaineering is a lifelong pursuit measured not in the accumulation of peaks attained but rather in a climber's willingness to keep moving forward toward the next goal. And often that means they must try and try again.

Unfortunately there wouldn't be time for another summit attempt on this trip. Even though they had enough provisions to remain on the mountain for another week, the team's permit was about to expire, and everyone had flights to catch. They had been on the mountain for twenty days, and it was time to head for home.

The following day they covered 8.5 miles, descending all the way back to their campsite at 7,800 feet. Though pleased with their performance as a team on the mountain, everyone still felt they had unfinished business left on Denali. Should the opportunity present itself again, each of them would gladly accept an invitation to give it another go. Given the ridiculously short memories mountaineers are known for, they would almost certainly have forgotten the danger they faced in the lightning storm if they were to make another attempt. Even as they hauled their packs and sleds back the way they had come, they each made a secret promise to themselves to one day return—and make it to the top.

POWERED BY GRAVITY, BUT ALSO BY THE DESIRE TO GET BACK HOME and the ease of lighter packs, the Expedition Denali team made swift work of the trip back down the mountain. Under a much less audacious burden, they could better enjoy the scenery and put the grand beauty of the Alaskan landscape into perspective. Less than forty-eight hours after dodging lightning bolts on the summit ridge, they found themselves safely back on the landing strip at 7,200 feet.

After a good night's sleep in the relatively oxygen-rich air, they packed their tents, reclaimed their emergency cache of supplies, and awaited the arrival of their plane. On the short return flight to civilization, they settled back into their seats to admire the view as it scrolled past them. They felt both nostalgic and proud as they watched the lofty slopes that had been their home fall away behind them. From the air, the mountains seemed unimaginably small, but from personal experience, they knew how grand and majestic they were. Those mountains held far more magic and mystery than could ever be seen from a distance.

When the team finally touched down on solid ground, the adventure came to a surprisingly abrupt end. As the cargo door slid open, the climbers were greeted by a warm breeze. Still in clothing suited to the glacier, they began shedding layers of Gore-Tex, down, and fleece even as their boots hit the tarmac. Walking on a surface not covered in ice and snow felt strange. But with each step, they put their time on the mountain farther behind them. As they penetrated more deeply into the civilized world, Denali became a vivid yet distant memory, a fantasy borne of dreams that had been realized and yet remained unfulfilled.

Back in Talkeetna, the team settled into a large table at a local pizza joint. As they ate steaming hot slices piled high with pepperoni, sausage, and fresh tomatoes and washed them down with cold beer, the climbers relished a meal that didn't involve melting snow into water. They raised their glasses in a toast to each other and themselves, their safe return, and the work still ahead.

Of everyone, DeBerry seemed the most anxious to get home. As soon as the school bus returned to the Farm, he got on his cell phone. After calling his wife and children, he began dialing up his air carrier in the hopes of getting the first flight out from Anchorage back to San Francisco. When Scott realized there was a chance for an early departure, he did what he could to change his ticket home as well.

The rest of the team, though no less eager to leave, settled into the chores of sorting and cleaning their gear. They each took long showers, relishing the feel of warm soapy water after so many days without it. Fresh from bathing, Rosemary decided that she had grown tired of her thick curly hair. With a towel wrapped around her shoulders, she sat down in one of the equipment bays and had Tyrhee use his grooming shears to shave her head completely bald. In the evening breeze of the Alaskan summer, Rosemary luxuriated in the cool relief of her bare skin.

In the hours before each member of the team boarded a plane for home, everyone seemed to find comfort and solace in their own special ways. After so many days in one another's company, they all wandered about the Farm on their own, reveling in the solitude. Billy immediately located his iPod from among his personal items and began playing his favorite music. Adina checked her email for an update on her job application. No word yet, but it seemed the documents had been received. DeBerry and Scott managed to get a flight out that night, so they hustled to pack their bags and board a shuttle to the airport. And Erica took a final tour of the Farm's library. As she perused the titles one last time, she felt proud of her accomplishments, confident that one day a book recounting her adventures in Alaska as a member of Expedition Denali would grace those shelves. Erica would get her happy ending.

Profile

Matthew Henson and Barbara Hillary

"The lure of the Arctic is tugging at my heart. To me the trail is calling! The old trail, the trail that is always new." **—Matthew Henson**

Though Barbara Hillary had no intention of actually purchasing a Rolls Royce, she couldn't help but admire it. There in the dealer showroom she paced its length from bumper to bumper, all its elegant chrome curves and gleaming black painted steel. She cast her gaze over the hood to the windshield and along the driver's side window where she peered in at the dark wood dashboard. More chrome glimmering on the elaborate dials winked back at her as she imagined her hands on the steering wheel, her foot on the gas pedal, the sound of the engine in her ears. Her reverie was broken when she caught site of a man in a dark suit with a white pocket square coming toward her. Staring up at him, she asked, "Can you please show me under the hood?"

The year was 1942 and Barbara Hillary was ten years old.

Barbara's father died before her second birthday and she was raised by a proud and demanding mother. Even though they had very little money, the Hillary family had a profound sense of dignity and self-respect that elevated Barbara's thinking and ambitions well beyond the circumstances of her existence.

"It was an asset that my mother raised us so that we didn't have a poverty mentality, and so I saw there was nothing wrong with going to the Rolls Royce showroom and learning all that I could," Barbara said. "It was the same with the American Museum of Natural History. I would go up to the library and see all these old people. Little did I know they were academics. I would go up and get books and everyone would be smiling. But I didn't know that it was unheard of for a Black kid to be in these halls of knowledge."

To this day Barbara credits her mother for instilling in her the critical importance of education, hard work, and discipline.

These values served Barbara well throughout her life. She trained at the Bellevue School of Nursing in New York City. Later in her career Barbara graduated from the New School University where she earned a bachelor's degree as well as a master's in professional studies with an emphasis on gerontology. She worked for many years at various nursing homes in the New York area, creating curriculum and training methods for staff development in facilities that serve the elderly. During her long and distinguished career as a nurse, she traveled extensively across the country whenever vacation time and her limited financial resources would allow. But when she retired at the age of sixty-two, Barbara's life as an adventurer finally came into full bloom.

Looking for experiences beyond her normal life at home in Queens, Barbara began to take short excursions into remote areas. Not being particularly fond of warm weather, she ventured into the wilderness regions of Manitoba, Canada, to photograph polar bears and learned how to cross-country ski. She also took lessons in how to handle a snowmobile, which eventually piqued her curiosity about other modes of snow terrain transportation. She even learned how to drive a dogsled.

"I became involved in northern travel and I fell in love with it," Barbara said. "And as a natural progression, I started to read about the North Pole, and much to my amazement I discovered that no Black woman or African-American woman had ever been to the North Pole.

Following that, the more I read the more I realized what a challenge it was and what a feat it would be if I were able to do it."

Through the course of her studies on the North Pole, Barbara became familiar with the first person to reach this Arctic objective. When Commander Robert Edwin Peary set out on his expedition in 1908, his company included 24 men, 19 sledges, and 133 dogs. After months of travel across a vast field of ice from the edge of Cape Sheridan on Ellesmere Island, one by one members of the party began turning back (which was part of the original plan). When the first human footprints where pressed into the snow at the northernmost point on the planet, all that remained of the original corps were Peary, 40 dogs, four native Inuit hunters, and an African-American man who would be forgotten by history for almost half a century.

Matthew Alexander Henson was born on August 8, 1866, one year after emancipation, to a family of freeborn sharecroppers in Nanjemoy, Maryland. When he was four, he and his family traveled north for better job prospects and settled in Washington, DC. Henson's mother died when he was seven, and his father passed away a few years later. Henson and his three sisters were left in the care of a cantankerous elderly uncle who treated the children with disdain and cruelty. When he was only eleven years old, Henson ran away from his home in DC and walked all the way to Baltimore, where he lived on the streets. He eventually found a job busing tables in a restaurant; the owner allowed Henson to sleep on the floor after closing time. Curled up on the damp wooden boards, he likely dreamed of a better life someplace far away.

A year later, Henson heard of a ship's captain looking for able-bodied men to crew a three-masted merchant sailing ship on a long voyage. With nothing to lose, he made his way to the docks and applied for a job aboard the *Katie Hines*. Though Henson was far too young and small to be any good as a common seaman, the captain, admiring the young man's spirit and determination, hired him on as a cabin boy. Over the next several years, under the mentorship of Captain Childs, Henson received an education, learned a variety of technical skills, became a competent sailor, and traveled the world, visiting Asia, North Africa, and the Black Sea.

When Captain Childs died in 1887, Henson took a job as a shop clerk for a furrier back in Washington, DC. Though his time at sea was a thing of the past, eighteen-year-old Henson was still very interested in a life of travel and adventure. So it was no small quirk of fate when a naval officer entered the shop one day to sell a collection of seal and walrus pelts that he had just obtained on an expedition to Greenland.

Impressed with Henson's experience and enthusiasm, Robert Peary hired him almost immediately as his personal assistant and invited him to take part in his next assignment. Serving in the Navy Corps of Civil Engineers, Peary had been tasked with mapping and exploring the jungles of Nicaragua in the hopes of creating a canal to connect the Atlantic Ocean with the Pacific. Henson and Peary spent the next two years traveling through the rainforests of Central America, a journey that would cement their friendship and bind their destinies.

In 1891, the two companions began an eighteen-year partnership of Arctic exploration that included the complete mapping of the Greenland ice cap. They discovered the great island's northernmost terminus. And during two expeditions in 1896 and 1897, they recovered three enormous meteor fragments, which they later sold to the American Museum of Natural History in New York for $40,000. The larger piece weighs thirty-one metric tons and is the third-largest intact meteor ever discovered and the heaviest ever transported by human beings. The funds supported several other expeditions over the next ten years.

While Peary was the public face of their partnership, Henson was the front man in the field. With his skills as a carpenter and craftsman, Henson personally built and maintained all of the sledges used on their expeditions. He was fluent in the Inuit language and established a rapport with the native people of the region. He came to be known by all he encountered as "Matthew the Kind One." Henson learned the methods the Inuit used to survive and travel through the incredibly hostile landscape of the Arctic. "He was more of an Eskimo than some of them," Peary once said. In addition, Henson was a very capable hunter, fisherman, and dog handler. And he trained even the most experienced of Peary's recruits on each of the eight attempts they made to reach the North Pole.

It's fair to suggest that much of Peary's success was the result of Henson's expertise. Though Peary repeatedly failed to reach his goal, he managed to return safely time and time again, having progressed a little farther with every trip. In 1906, with the support of President Theodore Roosevelt, Peary and Henson managed to get within 174 miles of the North Pole using a state-of-the-art ice breaker, a three-masted steam-powered schooner. "When my observations were taken," Peary wrote in his journal, "they showed that we had reached 87°6' north latitude, and had at last beaten the record, for which I thanked God."

Two years later, Peary and Henson would make their eighth and final attempt to reach the North Pole. Whether they succeeded or not, both men had decided this would be their last voyage together— by then in their forties, they could feel the strain of their long careers. A handpicked team sailed out of New York Harbor on July 6, 1908. The plan was to ferry and deposit loads of gear and food along the way, with each successive team of dog mushers returning to the ship that was iced into port at Ellesmere Island. A smaller team of two Americans and four Inuit companions would make the final push to their objective. Peary and Henson were the most likely choices to lead the North Pole team.

"Henson must go all the way," Peary said when they planned the trip months earlier. "I can't make it there without him."

The group arrived at their starting point at Cape Sheridan on September 5, 1908. There they spent the long Arctic winter assembling their supplies of meat. In February, Peary led the party by sledge to Cape Columbia, where he established a forward base camp on the ice. The expedition began in earnest when Henson led the first group of sledges toward the pole on March 1, 1909. For the next five weeks, the teams raced toward their goal.

In addition to temperatures that fell to sixty-five degrees below zero, they encountered cracking and drifting ice that formed patches of open water called "leads." But the group made steady progress, and the support teams gradually turned back as planned.

In his account of the adventure, *The Negro at the North Pole*, published in 1912, Henson made a detailed summary of the final five-day march to the pole. He, Peary, and four Inuits—Ooqueah, Ootah, Egingwah, and Seegloo—drove the five remaining dog sledges day after day for stretches that lasted twelve to fourteen hours. Moving quickly to avoid the possibility of a massive lead opening up behind them and blocking their way back home, they traveled more than 170 miles. By April 6, navigating by sexton and dead reckoning, they felt that their objective was finally within reach.

"We crawled out of our igloos and found a dense mist hanging over everything," he wrote. "Only at intervals, when the sun's rays managed to penetrate the mist, could we catch even a glimpse of the sky. Estimating the distance that we had come during the last four days, we figured that, unless something unusual happened to us during the course of this day, we should be at the Pole before its close."

According to his own recollection, Henson was in the lead sledge through much of the day, scouting the trail ahead.

"The Commander, who was about fifty yards behind, called out to me and said we would go into camp," wrote Henson. "We were in good spirits, and none of us were cold. So we went to work and promptly built our igloos, fed our dogs, and had dinner. The sun being obscured by the mist, it was impossible to make observations and tell whether or not we had actually reached the Pole. The only thing we could do was to crawl into our igloos and go to sleep."

The following day when the mist had cleared, Peary took measurements of their location relative to the position of the sun at the noon hour.

"The results of the first observation showed that we had figured out the distance very accurately, for when the flag was hoisted over the geographical center of the Earth, it was located just behind our igloos," Henson wrote.

The party had indeed reached the North Pole. But the question remained who had arrived there first. "I was in the lead that had overshot the mark by a couple of miles," Henson was quoted in a newspaper article upon their return. "We went back then, and I could see that my footprints were the first at the spot."

Upon their return to the United States, some reports in the press indicated that there was tension between Peary and Henson over who deserved credit for reaching the North Pole first. "From the time we knew we were at the Pole, Commander Peary scarcely spoke to me," Henson would later reveal. "It nearly broke my heart . . . that he would rise in the morning and slip away on the homeward trail without rapping on the ice for me, as was the established custom."

It seems odd that after such a long and successful partnership, the two men would become estranged from one another. It would be reasonable to give Peary and Henson equal credit for having reached the North Pole together as a team. But the racially divisive climate of the time would not permit an African-American man the same standing in the public eye for such a monumental feat of human achievement. So Peary was recognized as the first to reach the North Pole, while Henson was relegated to the role of sidekick. Despite Henson's indispensable contributions to their efforts for almost twenty years, he received hardly any acknowledgment.

The situation only worsened when Peary's claim of success was called into question. A man by the name of Frederick Cook professed to have reached the North Pole one year earlier on April 21, 1908. His claims quickly faded when several individuals came forward with compelling evidence to dispute Cook's contrived story. In the aftermath, however, many suggested that Peary had also failed to reach the North Pole. Several skeptics speculated that he missed the mark by several hundred miles. With few ways to verify the veracity of this kind of remote expedition, reports of success relied on the honor system. The only other person who could back up Peary's story was Henson, as the Inuit hunters didn't speak English. Though his testimony was likely deemed by many to be less than credible since he was a Black man, the strength of his character as substantiated by other members of the party carried a great deal of weight in affirming the truth of their journey to the top of the globe.

After returning from his last polar expedition, Peary was promoted to rear admiral and traveled the world for the rest of his life as an acclaimed hero. He died on February 20, 1920. But history would treat Matthew Henson much differently. Upon his return from the North

Pole, Henson took a job as a clerk with the federal customs house in New York City, on the recommendation of Theodore Roosevelt. He would spend the next thirty years leading a quiet life in relative seclusion. His contributions to the discovery of the North Pole went unrecognized until 1937, when the Explorers Club of New York made him an honorary member. In 1946, Henson was awarded a medal, identical to the one given to Peary, by the US Navy. And in 1954 President Dwight Eisenhower invited him to the White House to receive a special commendation for his early work as an explorer on behalf of the United States.

Henson died the following year on March 9, 1955. Though he was initially buried in Woodlawn Cemetery in the Bronx, his remains, along with those of his wife, were later relocated to Arlington National Cemetery. On the seventy-ninth anniversary of his trip to the pole, Henson was laid to rest with full military honors near the monument to Robert Peary. In 1996, an oceanographic survey ship was commissioned as the USNS *Henson* in his honor. And in 2000, the National Geographic Society presented Henson posthumously with its most prestigious award, the Hubbard Medal. Ironically, Robert Peary had been the first recipient of this prize in 1906.

Barbara Hillary knew of Henson, and his adventure piqued her interest. After suffering through bouts of both lung and breast cancer, she grew more determined than ever to continue to live her life to the fullest. So Barbara schemed to further dedicate the rest of her life to being an adventurer.

"I wanted to travel, but everyone kept handing me brochures for cruise ships," Barbara said. "I can't imagine anything more boring than sitting around for days on end with a bunch of boring married people. I wanted to go where I could see something unique, something special."

Having successfully beat cancer, Barbara set her sights on the most ambitious destination she could imagine.

"To get to the North Pole, the challenge starts when you make up your mind that you're going," she said. "It's a popular misconception that suddenly you're in the Arctic ice expanse and then everything starts to happen. No, the heaven and the hell of the adventure starts the day that you make up your mind that you're going. And by that I mean, who do you ask? After you tell someone you're going to the pole, can they tell you what to wear? How do you get there? All of the questions, the logistics, I found to be overwhelming, compounded with the fact that I had to organize and prepare the trip, basically all alone."

She freely admitted that her motivation had very little to do with any desire to demonstrate that a Black woman was no less capable of reaching the top of the world than anyone else. She wanted to make the trip to test the boundaries of her own abilities and her growth as a human being.

"Initially I had great racial pride and I still do. However, when I speak of growth, as I emerged and tried to constantly grow and constantly try to reach for maturity, because no one is really mature, it should be in my humble opinion a lifelong quest," she said. "And that's achieved by painful self-analysis, through struggle and challenging yourself, by going back to what works for you and defining your own yardstick."

It turned out the primary challenge for Barbara wasn't to convince *herself* that she could travel to the North Pole. The trick was convincing others.

"People would say to me, 'You're too old.' 'Black people don't like the cold.' 'With part of your lung missing, you won't be able to withstand the strain of exertion in all that frigid air.' One person actually said I'd be eaten alive by polar bears," she said. "I had to laugh and say, 'What? They don't cook you first?'"

But first she had to take care of the financial hurdle. As a retiree on a fixed income, she would have to rely on sponsors and donations to come up with the $23,000 to cover her base expenses.

"I was basically trying to sell an unknown product," she said. "Who is Barbara Hillary? What has she ever done? Why should we give her money to do this?"

Perhaps it was the notion of putting the first Black woman on the North Pole. Maybe some were intrigued by the idea of a seventy-five-year-old novice explorer with ambitions to accomplish such a monumental journey. But by 2007, Barbara had succeeded in raising the cash. As soon as she had the means, she left New York City and boarded a plane in Oslo bound for Svalbard, an archipelago in the Arctic Ocean off the coast of Norway. After a two-hour and forty-minute flight from Svalbard, Barbara landed in Barneo, a temporary outpost created each year by the Russian Geographical Society, and found herself in the middle of the Arctic summer. "One of the things I didn't account for in my planning was the twenty-four seven daylight," she said. "It messed with my mind a little bit to be wearing sunglasses at two in the morning."

The expedition company VICAAR operates a series of excursions from Barneo to the North Pole by skis, dog sledge, or helicopter. Accompanied by two guides, Barbara took a short helicopter flight to a spot near the pole and then skied the remaining distance to reach the North Pole on April 23, 2007.

"We just kept skiing and I said, 'Eugene, when are we going to reach the pole?' But he just kept ignoring me," Barbara said. "I was like a kid in the back seat of a car. Are we there yet? Are we there? And the more he ignored me the more I wanted to take that ski pole and hit him over the head. But then finally he turns to me and says, 'Barbara you're now standing on the top of the world.'"

Four years later Barbara made an equally ambitious journey, this time to the South Pole. But when she arrived in Chile in January of 2011 to make her way to Antarctica, she was stopped dead in her tracks by massive civil unrest in the region because the Argentinian government had increased the price of heating fuel. As a result the airports were blocked by round-the-clock demonstrations that put a halt to all air travel in or out of Punta Arenas for almost three weeks.

"You haven't lived until you're in a foreign country, you don't speak the language, and you start to run out of money," she said. "Every time I went to the dining room I started to peek in the kitchen to see how many dishes I'd have to wash."

By the time the demonstrations ended, the other travelers in her party had aborted their plans.

"I ended up being the only one going," Barbara said. So, along with a few of the research station's staff, Barbara boarded a giant Russian cargo plane that took her to the Antarctica base camp at Union Glacier, where she spent almost a week in an unheated tent— enduring temperatures and wind chills well below zero—waiting for a weather window to open. When the skies finally cleared, she boarded another plane and departed for Amundsen Station at the South Pole.

"It's important to understand that it wasn't just a leisurely plane trip. Every part of this journey was challenging," Barbara said. "And through all the waiting, it just seemed to drag on and on, and I just started asking myself, 'Do I really need this?' 'Do I need to subject myself to this?' 'Maybe it's time for me to go back.' But I just couldn't do it. I just couldn't do it because I knew that if I did, I would always ask myself, why didn't I stick it out another day?"

On June 6, 2007, the 110th Congress of the United States issued a resolution to acknowledge that Barbara Hillary was the first African-American woman to reach the North Pole. Having successfully reached the South Pole as well, Barbara is likely to be the only African-American woman to achieve both goals. And to those who would trivialize her accomplishments, Barbara, who at the age of eighty-three is planning her next expedition, defiantly suggests that they try it for themselves.

"If it were easy," she said, "More people would have done it."

Epilogue

Changing the Face of the Outdoors

Although they didn't reach the summit, Expedition Denali succeeded beyond its wildest dreams. As the different members of the team each went their separate ways, they began to disseminate what they learned. As of the summer of 2014, one year after the expedition, they'd gotten out in front of over eight thousand people, speaking to audiences ranging in size from twenty to four hundred. Billy was featured on the cover of *Sierra* magazine, as well as in the NOLS alumni magazine, the *Leader*. The expedition had been covered by media ranging from the *NBC Nightly News* to the *Huffington Post* to *Backpacker* magazine. The response has been overwhelmingly positive.

In early 2014, the team won the prestigious Outdoor Inspiration award from the Outdoor Industry Association. A documentary film about the expedition entitled *An American Ascent* premiered a few months later to a sold-out audience in Washington, DC. After the screening, the mother of one young man expressed her sincere gratitude to Expedition Denali for sharing this powerful story with her son. He "has been told many times what he 'can't do,' and he has defied the odds every time," she said. "I knew this film would grab him, and now he is very determined to do something similar."

Through the team's tireless efforts, they've gotten their message out there. Though there's no question there's a long way to go, thanks to the passion and determination of groups like this—and so many others who are toiling away in relative obscurity—there does indeed seem to be hope that we can make the wilderness a place that all people, no matter their race, can feel committed to preserving for future generations.

While the rest of the team went back to their respective professions, Scott took a job working with NOLS to manage the various presentations of the Expedition Denali story to schools and conservation groups across the United States. As in the work he did with Patagonia and other community outreach organizations, he was tasked with being a role model for young people. And even though he and his teammates did not make it to the summit, Scott fully appreciated the idea that the true value of their adventure was the journey itself.

"I know a lot of people say that, but I think it's really true. And I've said that from the very beginning, back when we all first met a year and a half ago," he said. "I was psyched to climb this mountain, but climbing the mountain was never the point. The fact that we each have these amazing stories and we have all been given this opportunity, we've taken charge, and we've come together as a team. That's a powerful story in itself. We can now go out and share our story with children. And that will inspire youth."

As successful as it was, Expedition Denali is only one of many steps needed to make a long-term difference in boosting the presence of minorities in the outdoors. It's heartening to know that several environmental groups across the country are working to find solutions and many are making real progress. In Los Angeles, Bill Vandenberg is an educator in the public school system who partners with the Sierra Club program Inner City Outings. He works with young people, mostly minorities, in Southern California to provide them with experiences in nature. Every year, Vandenberg takes a small group of kids on a series of day and overnight trips culminating in a backpacking adventure to Yosemite National Park.

"Those are the trips that most motivate the kids," he said. "And they're the ones who get inspired, go to college, and come back to the Sierra Club Youth Coalition as youth activists."

The Inner City Outings program engages more than fourteen thousand young people through fifty different volunteer organizations across the United States. Despite growing up in urban settings with very limited access to nature, these mostly African-American and Hispanic youths receive an opportunity to see the world from a different perspective.

"My experience working with kids is there's no exposure to the outdoors. That colors their perception. But once they're there, that all changes," Vandenberg said. "Stuff they've never imagined they could ever do, or would do, once they do it takes away all the preconceptions."

From these early interactions with young people, environmental organizations can then make the case for expanded programs toward life science education and ultimately careers in conservation. The San Francisco–based program NatureBridge provides hands-on learning opportunities at several national parks in California and Washington State for more than forty thousand students every year.

NatureBridge uses science education to give kids the background they need to understand why conserving the environment is important. And as the nation grows to include more people of color, the group's mission has expanded to include the education of future leaders who will decide the fate of public lands.

"We need to make sure that those folks have a connection because those people of color are the ones who are going to have to make the decision between whether we preserve public land or destroy it for the natural resources it provides," said Dr. Stephen Lockhart, board chairman of NatureBridge.

Even more advanced programs are now putting college students and recent grads into position to work full-time for the National Park Service. Vanessa Torres was formerly a ranger at Grand Teton National Park. In her role as youth and diversity coordinator, she was instrumental in creating a program that launched in 2011 called the Student Conservation Association's National Park Service Academy. Working in conjunction with the Teton Science School and the Student Conservation Association (SCA), the event drew twenty-nine students of racially diverse backgrounds from across the country.

"We were looking for students that had leadership skills, and who were interested in the outdoors and wanted to take on this kind of commitment," Torres said. "Not just committing their spring break, but committing to internships during the summer. We placed twenty-one of the twenty-nine students in summer jobs with the SCA or working for the National Park Service."

By creating a pool of qualified applicants from minority communities, programs like the National Park Service Academy are making a more diverse workforce possible. Torres, twenty-six, is a Latina who graduated from St. Mary's University with a bachelor's degree in political science and a master's in public administration. Though her family would prefer she had a more traditional job like working in a bank, Torres said she's getting the support she needs and takes great pride in her work.

"In my immediate and extended family, there's a lack of understanding of what I do," she said. "But now that I'm working on diversity issues, they're starting to get it because it's a little more like what I was doing in college. It's interesting how I've come full circle working on community and diversity outreach and coming here and doing the same thing in a national park."

Many like Torres believe that workforce diversity is vital to building a National Park Service that is more inclusive and inviting to the interests of minority visitors. And in order to do that, she says the service has to share examples of more employees that truly reflect the face of America.

WHILE GRASSROOTS ORGANIZATIONS ARE ONE VITAL TACTIC FOR increasing minority youth's exposure to the outdoors, there's no denying the power of celebrity. When Yosemite National Park Ranger Shelton Johnson was told to expect several African-American women who were about to have their first overnight outdoor experience, he never expected Oprah Winfrey and her friend Gayle King to show up for a night in the great outdoors.

Their trip became the spotlight of two episodes of the *Oprah Winfrey Show*, and Johnson was flown to Chicago to appear in the studio audience. With two hours of high-profile television devoted to boosting the national parks to a mainstream minority audience, Johnson hopes that more people, particularly people of color, will be inspired to visit and thoroughly embrace these wild scenic places for the national treasures they are.

"Oprah has the ability to influence trends in travel and where people go on vacation," Johnson said. "But she didn't just visit a national park. What made this special was that she was camping. She didn't do the Ahwahnee Hotel. She's a billionaire and she went camping."

Rue Mapp is the founder of Outdoor Afro, a nonprofit dedicated to the promotion of outdoor recreation to underrepresented communities. "We know that women are the gatekeepers of experience for their families. So unless you get moms engaged and invested, getting people of color into the outdoors won't be sustainable," Mapp said. "Oprah getting out there camping as an African-American woman is showing that it's possible. And that opening is what we need to further the dialog. I don't care if she does it in stilettos. She's out there doing it."

While today there are no barriers like the Jim Crow segregation laws of the 1950s and '60s that keep Black Americans out of parks, there remain several uncodified cultural limitations that discourage people of color from spending time outdoors or pursuing careers in outdoor recreation, conservation, or wilderness advocacy. As a people, we seem to possess an unsubstantiated belief that we don't belong. And so we stay away. But the barriers blocking us from nature are not in the real world. They're in our own minds.

With the right role models, encouragement, access to information, and positive exposure, there's really no reason why more people of color can't spend time in nature. But we need to get over our own mind-set. With any luck, the Expedition Denalis and Oprahs of this world—along with the hard work of many people and new programs—can help get us there and help us further bridge the adventure gap.

New Afterword

A Decade of Progress Toward Something Yet Higher

When Expedition Denali concluded, few believed that was the end of the story. Subsequently, the enduring narrative of Black adventurers has only grown richer and more diverse. Ten years have passed since the team safely returned to their families and communities to inspire a new generation of explorers. Even now, the impact of this remarkable journey continues to drive the imaginations of those, like Charles Crenchaw, in search of "something yet higher."

For the record, shortly after the team retreated from the Football Field at more than 19,000 feet that June, there *was* a successful Black summit of Denali. As part of The North Face team led by Conrad Anker, veteran climber Philip Henderson made a second attempt. Once the storm had passed the next day, Henderson and the five members of his original crew climbed from their camp at 14,200 feet all the way to the summit.

"We were lucky to have the extra time we needed to finish the climb. We were already overdue, and everyone else had to get back," Henderson later told me. "Even after we came down, we had to wait out another storm for about five or six days at base camp."

I never intended to leave Henderson's success out of this story. Though we've known each other for many years, he had never mentioned his second summit bid, and I'd never thought to ask. I'd felt satisfied with the original narrative of survival in the face of adversity. It was only as Henderson and I were discussing his future plans a few years ago that he told me about the events that followed Expedition Denali's retreat from the summit. Henderson has emerged as a key character in this continuing story, bringing the adventure forward with something even more significant when he, along with a few members of the Expedition Denali team, made history on Mount Everest.

After our wonderful adventure in Alaska, I can look back over the past decade with pride and awe at how much has been accomplished. By the summer of 2014, one year after the expedition, the team members were invited to various events across the country, appearing in front of thousands of people. They shared slideshows at speaking engagements with audiences ranging in size from twenty to four hundred. Billy Long was featured on the cover of *Sierra Magazine* and in the NOLS alumni publication, *The Leader.* Media organizations—from NBC Nightly News to the *Huffington Post* to *Backpacker Magazine*—covered stories on the expedition. The response from audiences and readers was overwhelmingly positive. Despite the unfortunate pushback we received from folks who believed the expedition was unnecessary or overrated, people in communities across the country were excited to hear our compelling story.

Later that same year, the team won the prestigious Outdoor Inspiration Award from the Outdoor Industry Association, and we produced a documentary called *An American Ascent* with Wild Vision Films. In 2015, Expedition Denali team members Billy Long, Rosemary Saal, and Tyrhee Moore journeyed to Washington, DC, along with me and the film's co-producer and writer Andy Adkins. In a private screening for almost two hundred high school students and representatives from several youth-focused nonprofit organizations, we presented our story at the White House.

Although I never admitted it out loud, I secretly hoped that our mountaineering adventure would pique the interest of President Barack

Obama. Unfortunately, heartbreaking headlines throughout that week made a personal visit with the commander-in-chief impossible. On June 17, 2015, nine parishioners at the Emanuel African Methodist Episcopal Church in Charleston, South Carolina, were shot and killed by a racially motivated terrorist during a bible study. Among those slain was Reverend Clementa Pinckney, the pastor of the church and a former South Carolina state senator. The murders drew the nation's attention to more important matters. On the day of our film screening, President Obama was scheduled to give the eulogy at the funeral of Reverend Pinckney. The sad irony of these circumstances clearly illustrates why expressions of Black representation like Expedition Denali are still so profoundly necessary in twenty-first-century America.

In the state where the first shots of the Civil War were fired at Fort Sumter, the Confederate battle flag still flew over its capitol. As Reverend Pinckney's funeral procession rolled slowly past South Carolina's state capitol building where he once served, both the flags of the United States and the State of South Carolina were lowered to half-mast in his honor. But by state law, the flag of the Confederacy could not be taken down for any reason, including the death of one of the community's most prominent Black dignitaries. We had hoped to celebrate Expedition Denali with President Obama. Instead, while we screened our film, he sang "Amazing Grace" in front of a grieving crowd and a troubled nation.

Our team gathered at the Eisenhower Executive Office Building that adjoins the White House. As the events in the film unfolded, the young people in the audience, mostly people of color, sat watching, their attention riveted. We proudly shared our story on stage to an auditorium of wide-eyed future explorers. Afterward, we fielded several questions about the expedition and the prospects of getting more people of color into the outdoors. But the query of one young man in particular made the entire project—everything we had done over the previous four and half years—completely worthwhile:

"Do you think I can do something like that one day?"

I believe that our message was a resonant echo of an emerging spirit of discontent that was sweeping the nation. Mere hours after our screening, a Black American woman named Bree Newsome climbed the flagpole at the South Carolina State House in Charleston to remove the Confederate flag. Outraged by the insult to Reverend Pinckney during his funeral procession, she took a stand by climbing. In a rebellious act of defiance, she unclipped the banner of hate and brought it down.

"We can't continue like this another day," Newsome demanded. "It's time for a new chapter where we are sincere about dismantling white supremacy and building toward true racial justice and equality."

Prepared to face the consequences and be arrested, Newsome did what she believed was right. Taking precautions for safety with a helmet and climbing gear, she made a bold statement, encouraging others to follow their passion despite fear and apprehension in the face of vocal or even violent opposition. When she reached the ground, Newsome was taken into custody by police officers. Though the flag was put back in place an hour later, this act of civil disobedience stood for all to see as an enduring expression of nonviolent protest. Within a month, the state of South Carolina passed legislation to permanently remove the Confederate flag.

By sharing our film at the White House, we represented the effort to make the outdoors accessible to everyone, as well as encourage the interests of environmental protection among underrepresented communities of color. We can only hope that by encouraging more people to cross the adventure gap, we can inspire a new generation of social activists like Bree Newsome to defy the boundaries of convention and outdated traditions steeped in discrimination. Perhaps we can encourage this new generation to boldly stand in support of efforts to mitigate the negative impacts of climate change and preserve the integrity of the natural resources that so many of us enjoy.

Expedition Denali was part of an emerging awareness of the importance of encouraging diversity, equity, and inclusion across the United States. The Black Lives Matter movement was established in 2013. In the years that followed, progress continued in addressing the disparities of social and environmental justice in all avenues of American life, including managing our public lands and interpreting our national heritage through our parks and monuments.

In September 2015, President Obama signed an executive order to formally change the name of Mount McKinley to Denali. The following year, he became the first president of the United States to visit Yosemite Valley since John F. Kennedy in 1962. His administration's White House Council on Environmental Quality met regularly with environmental organizations that advance the interests of people of color in outdoor recreation.

In 2016, to mark the one-hundredth anniversary of the National Park Service, a group known as the Next 100 Coalition was formed to inspire social change into the next century. The collaboration included Outdoor Afro, Natives Outdoors, the Greening Youth Foundation, Latino Outdoors, Diverse Environmental Leaders, GreenLatinos, and many others, including my organization, The Joy Trip Project. As a result of our efforts, President Obama issued a presidential memorandum to the National Park Service and other public land agencies on January 12, 2017. This document, called "Promoting Diversity and Inclusion in Our National Parks, National Forests, and Other Public Lands and Waters," encourages park stewards to advocate for a more inclusive and complete story of America. It pushes for diverse voices in the decision-making process for new publicly managed recreation sites. And it recommends increasing the number of outreach programs dedicated to providing access to natural spaces for diverse communities.

Unfortunately, many of the advances made during the Obama administration were slowly eroded under the presidency of Donald Trump. At an Oval Office meeting in March 2017, the newly inaugurated chief executive asked Alaska's two US senators, Lisa Murkowski and Dan Sullivan, if they would like him to reverse the executive order of his predecessor and change the name Denali back to Mount McKinley. "Lisa—Sen. Murkowski—and I jumped over the desk," Sullivan told CNN. "We said no, no!"

We can all be grateful that Denali remains the name of the highest peak in North America. But Trump went on to institute a variety of policies prohibiting federal agencies from implementing the programs of the previous administration that encouraged diversity, equity, and inclusion in the management of public land.

Fortunately, he was too late. Because of initiatives like Expedition Denali and others led by dozens of racial affinity groups, including members of the Next 100 Coalition, the movement to bring more people of color into the outdoors was well underway. As white supremacists rallied with torches in Charlottesville, Virginia, chanting, "You will not replace us" in 2017, groups like Brothers of Climbing, Flash Foxy, and Brown Girls Climb were hosting meetups across the South and the Northeast at indoor climbing gyms and outdoor bouldering areas. These organizations were changing the face of the outdoors by showing up and unapologetically embracing the sport of climbing as their own.

"Events like our Color the Crag Climbing Festival are another way we do that. We are the future of the sport whether the industry wants to admit it or not," said Brothers of Climbing co-founder Mikhail Martin. "We are the trendsetters in other areas of pop culture, and I think the same is going to happen in climbing. We want to bring a little soul into climbing."

Out west, Black and brown athletes started arriving with ropes, carabiners, and harnesses in the most popular climbing areas across the region, including Joshua Tree, Bishop, Moab, and Yosemite. Organizations like Climbers of Color, based in Seattle, began offering courses in placing anchors, wilderness first aid, glacier travel, and crevasse rescue. These affinity groups helped increase representation and visibility, leading to a growing number of people of color training for attempts on peaks such as Mount Rainier in Washington State and, of course, Denali in Alaska. Among them was Rosemary Saal.

As a professional mountain guide and the youngest female member of Expedition Denali, Rosemary had built her skills to become an expedition leader in her own right. In 2018, she and Philip Henderson were invited to lead a trip for Outdoor Afro to climb Mount Kilimanjaro in Tanzania. They made history by putting the first all-Black American team of climbers on the summit of the highest peak on the African continent. A few weeks after their return, I had the privilege of moderating a panel discussion with a few of the expedition members at the Outdoor Retailer show in Denver.

"We see these types of panels all the time, major mountaineers telling their stories, which can tend to be unrelatable, or the goal seems so far out of reach," said team member and Brown Girls Climb cofounder Bethany Leavitt. "Having the team tell their stories from the highs and lows really showed everyone that they could explore this mountain. We don't really call ourselves mountaineers, just people who like to climb mountains."

Like Expedition Denali, the Outdoor Afro summit of Mount Kilimanjaro raised awareness of high-altitude mountaineering to communities of color. This level of visibility alters the perception of what a mountaineer looks like. In so doing, more people are beginning to see themselves in those roles. As the number of Black and brown climbers and other adventure athletes continues to multiply, the face of the outdoors is indeed changing.

With this transformation also comes a reckoning. The American people are being encouraged to understand that the lack of diversity in the outdoors—the adventure gap—is a glaring reflection of the larger racial disparities in our society. Since Expedition Denali and the start of the Black Lives Matter movement, social and environmental justice issues have followed parallel paths, often intersecting.

On February 23, 2020, a twenty-five-year-old Black man named Ahmaud Arbery was jogging through a suburban neighborhood near Atlanta, Georgia, when three white men, including one who was a former police officer, murdered him. On March 13, Breonna Taylor, a twenty-six-year-old Black woman, was sleeping in her Louisville, Kentucky, apartment when a no-knock search warrant led to her being fatally shot by white police officers. On May 25, George Floyd, a Black resident of Minneapolis, was arrested on a public street for a minor infraction when a white police officer murdered him. Within hours of that incident, a Black man named Christian Cooper was bird-watching in New York City's Central Park when he was falsely accused of threatening the life of a white female dog walker.

Each of these incidents shares a blatant disregard for the safety of Black Americans in places where they had every right to be. These individuals also experienced the severe overreaction of white people with the presumption of authority to exact lethal force. Public outrage over these events, and others like them, across the country in 2020 prompted many organizations and institutions to ramp up their commitment to better serve and engage with communities of color. In the outdoor recreation industry, that initiative included acknowledging the long-term effects of racial discrimination in public lands management and renewing an effort to actively build unobstructed access to the natural environment.

"We should recognize that systemic racism exists on both the streets of our cities and inside our national parks," wrote cultural geographer Dr. Carolyn Finney in the *Guardian* on June 3, 2020. "We have to see full representation at every level in the environmental sector, and we need power structures to shift so that Black and brown people are shaping policies and our national conversations."

More authentic representation of people of color in the outdoor recreation space has increased. Feature magazine articles and short films now regularly depict Black and brown outdoor adventurers as both talented athletes *and* social activists. Through our own agency and initiative, we are making great strides not only in diversity, equity, and inclusion but also in leadership.

In 2022, Philip Henderson successfully organized and managed the first all-Black expedition to the summit of Mount Everest, the highest peak in the world. Called the Full Circle Everest Expedition, his team of ten climbers included former Expedition Denali climbers Rosemary Saal and James "K.G." Kagambi, with Adina Scott coordinating logistics at base camp. The other members of the team were Manoah Ainuu, Eddie Taylor, Demond "Dom" Mullins, Thomas Moore, and Evan Green. The remaining members of the group who made it to Camp 3 with Henderson were Fred Campbell and Abby Dione. The local guides, whose assistance was vital to the expedition's success, were Pasang Nima Sherpa, Lhakpa Sonam Sherpa, Phurtemba Sherpa, Dawa Chhiri Sherpa,

Sonam Gyalje Sherpa, Nima Nuru Sherpa, Chopal Sherpa, Chawang Lhendup Sherpa, Tasha Gyalje Sherpa, and Amrit Ale. Still images and video were captured by Pemba Sherpa and Nawang Tenji Sherpa.

It's paramount we acknowledge the names and roles of all the people involved in this and other monumental endeavors. Too often, we neglect the contributions of those who played a supporting role or even a critical part in the successful outcome of groundbreaking events. Not only is this a remarkable achievement in the history of high-altitude mountaineering, but as the first Everest expedition orchestrated and executed by people of color, it also marks another step forward in the global advancement of racial diversity, equity, and inclusion in the outdoor recreation industry.

From the growth we have seen since Expedition Denali, we can now imagine new opportunities for people of color to become more firmly established as professionals in the outdoor business. In spaces once predominated by white athletes, product designers, marketing executives, and media producers, we are now seeing the emergence of talented individuals who identify as Black, Indigenous, or people of color. As their stories begin to take center stage, the industry can better address the cultural interests of a much more diverse audience. Today these outdoor professionals of color are leading the way toward expanding the representation of many different identities in adventure sports through storytelling and popular media.

Commercial photographer Stan Evans, for example, believes that now is the moment to promote equality in the outdoors by emulating the success of other industries such as entertainment, art, music, and fashion. "Where are the diverse creators, the leaders of styles and trends? What if we studied those spaces and mixed that ethos with the outdoor business?" he said in an email exchange. "Understanding that value and what it can bring to the outdoor industry allows us the confidence to sit equally at any table and then add our own cultural and artistic narratives."

With so many ways to present the outdoors to this expanded audience, the outdoor industry can only grow larger and more innovative. "For a long time, this industry has had its stories only from a particular perspective. I didn't even see myself," said media producer L. Renee Blount. "And there are so many stories that need to be retold. By inviting more people to the party to tell it, the narratives will get so much richer—more flavor, more sizzle, more examples of what's possible."

At the head of their own production companies, creative people of color are now in the driver's seat to manage not only the scope of their visions but also their budgets. As project leaders, they tell more stories, but also support the production crews and athletes from the communities they aim to serve. "We try to make sure our film teams are reflective of the folks in front of the camera and as diverse as they are talented," said adventure film producer and director Faith Briggs. "When I look at my collaborators, I feel very proud of who I've been able to hire and the projects I've been able to assist others in making."

Expedition Denali set an example for what is possible when people of color intentionally create opportunities for themselves and others to become better represented in the continuing story of outdoor recreation. The progress that has been made over the last ten years demonstrates the long journey toward lasting change. Each passing moment that encourages a new expedition, a new film, a new story, or a book in which Black and brown people can see themselves as part of the natural world is just another step forward in closing the adventure gap.

Expedition Denali Team Members

Where Are They Now?

Ten years after safely returning home from their climb, the members of Expedition Denali have gone on to lead remarkable lives. Their experience in Alaska helped guide the direction of their careers with a continued commitment to community service. Each of them still represents the admirable qualities of perseverance and self-discipline they displayed on the mountain.

As the team's youngest member, **TYRHEE MOORE** perhaps represents the project's most enduring achievement. He's closest in age to the emerging generation the expedition most wanted to reach, and he went on to climb other mountains. In addition to a second ascent of Denali, Tyrhee has climbed Aconcagua in South America and Mount Kilimanjaro in Africa. Inspired to give others in his Washington, DC, community the same opportunities he had, Tyrhee formed a nonprofit organization called Soul Trak. Through various programs ranging from rock climbing to kayaking to mountain biking, this organization provides hands-on learning experiences for people of color in outdoor spaces.

"Being part of Expedition Denali, we were dreaming really big! We didn't know what would come of this, and I don't think we can necessarily take credit for every aspect of it, but to see where we are now is unbelievable to me," Tyrhee said. "Ten years is not that much time to make the amount of progress the community has made, especially with so much working against us. I've just been thoroughly impressed to see how much visibility a lot of these issues have started to make."

When **ERICA WYNN** joined the expedition, she took a leave of absence from college. Upon her return from Alaska, she reenrolled in school and earned a bachelor's degree from American University in Washington, DC. She has since worked at several nonprofit organizations that assist young people in college preparation and placement. In her current position at Matriculate, based in New York City, Erica trains and supports college advisors who primarily serve low-income high school juniors and seniors. She hopes to one day earn a master's degree in social work.

Though she had the least experience in the outdoors among her expedition teammates, Erica still finds joy and solace in nature and leads day trips for the outdoor engagement organization called GirlTrek. "It's still fun for me to think about ways that public health and mental health interact with how we can use outdoor spaces and activities like hiking to help take care of our minds and bodies," she said. "Even if I don't do this in a formal way, when I have kids, who will be Black, they will be part of a new generation of folks of color who are connected to the outdoors. If not for Expedition Denali, NOLS courses, and GirlTrek, if I hadn't had the opportunity to go through those things, that might not be the case."

Also based in New York City, **BILLY LONG** continued his career as a bartender and eventually opened a pizza restaurant called Parkside in the Flatbush neighborhood. Billy shared that he underestimated how much time and commitment it would take to run a busy establishment, so he slowly transitioned out of the service industry and started training in computer programming. When the COVID-19 pandemic hit in 2020, he utilized the lockdown for studying. With an entirely new skill set, he now works for a digital design firm called CMYK.

Even with the peaks and valleys of entrepreneurship and career changes, Billy still has had opportunities to continue climbing. He completed a winter ascent of Mount Washington in New Hampshire. On the way down, he spent an evening at the Harvard Cabin, a mountaineering lodge at the base of Huntington Ravine. Though he is a devout urbanite today, he attributes his happiness and success to those months he spent climbing in Alaska. "I wouldn't be who I am today without Expedition Denali. It's hard to quantify how that's true, but I would not be," Billy said. "I've been trying to, in some way, explain that to people because it feels so inspiring to me. But I don't know how to say it because I don't know how I am different. I just know that I am. I wouldn't be this human being without that experience."

The oldest member of Expedition Denali, **STEPHEN SHOBE**, is as active and vibrant as ever. Now a retired AT&T line technician, he continues to install cable systems and radio towers freelance. Shobe also runs an international travel agency with his wife, Jane, which they opened in 2019. Despite the impact of the pandemic, they operate tours in exotic destinations such as Tahiti and Belize, where Shobe indulges his love of scuba diving.

He still aspires to mountaineering projects but on a less ambitious scale. With a luxury cruise ship that stops in Antarctica, he hopes to climb Mount Vinson of the Seven Summits one day. "But that will be just for me. There won't be a movie or anything like that," he said. "I just want to keep diving and traveling. You know, enjoying life and doing what I can to stay young, fit, and healthy."

ADINA SCOTT has worked in the Southern Hemisphere for the US Antarctic Program since returning from Denali in 2013. She is the marine computer and instrumentation specialist aboard two ships, the ARSV *Laurence M. Gould* and the RV *Nathaniel B. Palmer*, icebreakers used for research by the National Science Foundation. Though she spends weeks and sometimes months at sea, her home base is in Leavenworth, Washington, where she occasionally plays mandolin and fiddle with a folk band called the Chumlilies.

Her technical expertise with computers, plus her mountaineering experience, made Adina the perfect candidate to manage logistics for the 2022 Full Circle Everest Expedition. Adina made the trek to base camp and kept lines of communication open between the climbers and their supporters back home. Looking back on her time in Alaska a decade ago, she sees the progress of diversity and representation in adventure sports as part of an ongoing evolution of culture.

"I think Expedition Denali was part of the growth that was coming up from more and more people of color getting involved in the outdoors. A lot of Black and brown folks in urban areas were being exposed to climbing through local rock gyms," Adina said. "We definitely helped create more representation, but the culture seemed to be moving in that direction already. Just look at where we are now."

STEPHEN DEBERRY is still a Silicon Valley entrepreneur with an eye on social change and environmental justice. He runs the Bronze Venture Fund, which creates economic prosperity in communities that have long been subjected to inequitable treatment through systemic racism. By applying the principles of anthropology and sound financial planning, DeBerry helps correct the many disparities in Black and brown neighborhoods, advising conscious choices that are in the best interests of *everyone*, rather than the privileged few.

"The vast inequities between communities are unnatural and unnecessary. It's an artifact of bad design and a false choice," he said in his 2018 East Palo Alto TED Talk. "The good news is it doesn't have to be this way. We live in a time of new tools to solve old problems."

Team member **RYAN MITCHELL** has continued his athletic ambitions but at lower altitudes. Based in upstate New York, he runs competitively in USA Track and Field events ranging from the 800 meter to the 5K. In 2019, he finished second in his age group at the national championships in the 1500 meter with a time of 04:34.35. When he's not on the track, he still enjoys hiking through the Adirondack or Catskill Mountains. As a professor of chemistry and nutrition, Ryan splits his time teaching at Russell Sage College and Hudson Valley Community College, impressing upon young people the importance of a healthy diet and physical exercise, preferably outdoors.

"I do what I can to encourage them to not be shy about exploring different ways to get outside," Ryan said. "Because I teach nutrition and wellness quite broadly, I try to put my money where my mouth is, so to speak. It's one thing to talk about wellness and staying fit. It's another thing to get out there and make a big effort. And Expedition Denali was a big effort."

As the founder and director of the nonprofit WeGotNext, **SCOTT BRISCOE** inspires younger generations in the San Francisco Bay Area to build empowering relationships with the natural world. His organization provides mentoring opportunities for people of color to share their stories of environmental stewardship for the benefit of others in their community. Through a team of ambassadors—from fly-fishers to mountaineers—WeGotNext expands on the vision of Expedition Denali with role models who effect lasting change through their love of nature.

"We have the opportunity to remind people that their connection to the natural world is real, it exists, and they too have a say in whether or not a pipeline should be placed close to local water supplies, or a wildlife refuge should be compromised for fossil fuel development," Scott wrote for the Patagonia blog *The Cleanest Line*. "It is an opportunity to collectively come together across the divisions that persist. For me, it has been all the young girls and boys I've met who were looking for some inspiration to get outdoors."

In the years since 2013, **ROSEMARY SAAL** continued her training as a mountaineer and became an outdoor educator for NOLS. She frequently leads trips through the western ranges of the United States and as far away as New Zealand. Recruited to be part of the 2018 Outdoor Afro expedition to Tanzania, she co-led the first all-Black American ascent of Mount Kilimanjaro. As a member of the 2022 Full Circle Everest Expedition in Nepal, she became the second Black American woman to reach the summit of the highest mountain in the world. When she's not climbing, Rosemary enjoys her work as a barista at a local coffee shop near her home in Sacramento, California.

"It is so powerful to have the representation, to have these historic moments, especially for Black climbers doing big things, climbing Denali and Mount Everest. Doing these traditionally hard things that very few people get to do is important," Rosemary said. "It's also so important to accept and embrace that there can be moments, big and small, accomplishments big and small. I want to have a balance. I want to keep pushing the envelope. And hopefully pushing the envelope in these big ways allows more and more folks in the Black community to just embrace being free and finding joy and living life in the small ways as well."

Finally, the mastermind behind Expedition Denali, **APARNA RAJAGOPAL-DURBIN**, deserves a great deal of recognition. After years as a field instructor, she became the first diversity, equity, and inclusion manager for NOLS, spearheading the initiative that brought the nine climbers together in Alaska. A few years later, in 2015, Aparna left NOLS to create the Avarna Group, a consulting firm that advises environmentally focused organizations. Her clients include more than 350 outdoor education camps, specialty retailers, equipment manufacturers, trade associations, universities, and municipalities. She and her partners offer training and guidance to these institutions in implementing diversity, equity, and inclusion practices into all aspects of their business, including public engagement.

"I think the work that it takes is cultural change, helping those on the margins to have a sense of belonging. The work is making sure people have positive experiences in public lands and recreation in organizations," Aparna said. "And if we keep focusing on their experiences and believing in their stories, I think that is hopefully the future. I can't be hopeless. I owe it to my seven generations from now to have hope. Hopelessness is a failure of imagination. And we have to have hope to engage in that radical imagination and make change."

Acknowledgments

AS THIS BOOK IS THE CULMINATION OF MY LIFE'S WORK (SO FAR), IT IS only fitting that I acknowledge first the hundreds of outdoor retailers, gear and clothing manufacturers, and wilderness education professionals who so warmly welcomed me and encouraged me to explore this wonderful world of adventure that I love so much. Each of them helped me across the gap between apprehension and ambition in more ways than they can ever imagine. I especially want to thank my good friend and former boss Malcolm Daly, the founder of climbing equipment company Trango, who introduced me to the story of Charles Crenchaw. Without Malcolm's help, this courageous mountaineer might still be lost in the pages of history.

Since I made the transition from salesman to journalist, I've had the pleasure of working with many talented and supportive editors. I want to especially thank those who encouraged my work on the topic of diversity in outdoor recreation. Steve Paulson, executive producer of Wisconsin Public Radio's *To the Best of Our Knowledge*, gave me an excellent start by airing my piece on the Buffalo Soldiers in 2009. Jodi Peterson, the editor of *High Country News*, commissioned a series of short articles in 2010 and 2011 for her magazine's blog "A Just West"—these stories followed my journey through six national parks in search of African-American outdoor enthusiasts and their use of public lands. Several of those interviews inform the narrative of this book. Katie Ives, the editor in chief at *Alpinist*, published my first story on Charles Crenchaw as well as a profile of Everest climber Sophia Danenberg in

2012. Her meticulous editing and fact-checking support brought my work to the attention of Mountaineers Books, whose editor in chief Kate Rogers commissioned this piece of historical nonfiction.

Kate, having championed this book through every stage of its development from start to finish, is the unsung hero of this story. With just the right amount of cajoling and tough love, she rallied my enthusiasm for this project through some pretty dark moments of writer's block and an overabundance of material to create a clear and compelling narrative. Thanks for putting up with my whining, Kate!

Along with editing assistance from Jenna Free, Christina Henry de Tessan, and Erin Moore, I got a lot of help from several key individuals whose contributions shaped this story. A surviving member of the 1964 McKinley Expedition, Ed Boulton, provided first-person information on the life and character of Charles Crenchaw. Lowell Skoog at the Seattle Mountaineers History Committee Archives provided several historic photographs as well as a copy of the expedition log. Librarians Alex Depta and Beth Heller at the American Alpine Club were incredibly helpful in locating many of the historic documents on record. And Dr. Nina Roberts at San Francisco State University was vital in quantifying much of the social science information used in identifying some of the underlying causes of the adventure gap. (Sadly, Dr. Nina, as she was known, passed away in 2022.)

The information behind the Buffalo Soldiers story came to life with the help of ranger Shelton Johnson. In addition to writing the foreword to this book, he helped me to understand the importance of the role these valiant men played in the creation of Yosemite and the rest of the National Park System. By preserving their memory, Johnson has done each of us a great service. His thoughtful stewardship of this important legacy has inspired many of my projects over the last several years, including this one.

The genius behind Expedition Denali is the remarkable work of the dedicated professionals at the National Outdoor Leadership School. The brainchild of Aparna Rajagopal-Durbin, this audacious project was supported by public relations manager Jeanne O'Brien—these two incredible women pulled the team of climbers and support staff together to make the 2013 ascent of Denali possible. Over the course of eighteen months, they organized everything from training missions to slideshows that told this inspiring story of adventure. I can only hope that I have done justice to their monumental efforts to make history.

This project would not have been possible without the financial assistance of my sponsors. The outdoor equipment company Patagonia provided me with the resources to work on the road for months at a time while gathering information and materials to tell this very complicated story. I am grateful to Rob Bondurant for backing my every move. MAKO Surgical Corporation not only provided me with the prosthetic implants to replace my failed hips, but also contributed funds to keep me on my feet and working in Alaska throughout the expedition. Special thanks to my talented surgeon, Dr. Richard Illgen at the University of Wisconsin Hospital, and to Amy Cook of AMC Public Relations for arranging a grant from MAKO without which this book would never have been completed.

Early drafts of the manuscript were proofread by my very good friend and neighbor Jennifer Harrington. Her eye for detail helped to spare my editors the agony of horrendous spelling and grammar errors. She also offered suggestions to make the narrative more accessible to a general audience of nonclimbers.

The Adventure Gap narrative includes the stories of many remarkable individuals who shared with me, and now the readers of this book, the intimate details of their personal lives. Each profile is the result of several interviews collected over the course of the past five years. For their faith in my discretion and commitment to getting their stories straight, I want to thank esteemed filmmaker Ken Burns, aspiring National Park Service employee Dwayne Smallwood, mountaineer Sophia Danenberg, professional snowboarder Ryan Hudson, champion sport climber Kai Lightner, and Expedition Denali NOLS instructors Aaron Divine and Robby ReChord. This list also includes polar explorer Barbara Hillary, who passed away in 2019 at age 88, after the original edition of this book was published, and who remained feisty and inspiring until the end.

Obviously, this book would not have been possible without the generous cooperation, collaboration, and friendship extended to me by the members of the Expedition Denali team. I am grateful for their support and inspired by their collective strength, courage, and resolve. Thank you Adina, DeBerry, Rosemary, Billy, Ryan, Tyrhee, Scott, Erin, and Shobe.

And finally I owe the greatest debt of gratitude to my beautiful and loving wife, Shamane. With a busy writing schedule of her own as a daily news reporter, as well as an active calendar of athletic events, she is a constant grounding influence in my life who keeps my otherwise ill-conceived flights of fancy from spiraling out of control. By making a comfortable home for me to come back to after weeks of glacier travel or chasing climbers across half the continent, she is an ever-present reminder of why all summits are optional and safe returns are mandatory.

Resources

In the decade since Expedition Denali many resources have emerged to help develop the basic principles of diversity, equity, and inclusion in outdoor recreation and environmental conservation. Originally compiled by Dr. Don Rakow of Cornell University and Laura Brown of the University of Connecticut, the "Anti-Racism in the Outdoors (ARITO) Guide" started out as an annotated list of articles and online content references that explore the complex issues of racial disparities in the equitable access of all people to the outdoors.

Through the work of the Joy Trip Project, Together Outdoors, and other partners, the ARITO Guide has since amassed a more comprehensive—though by no means exhaustive—database of organizations, media, and affinity groups. New groups, educators, activists, podcasts, and more continue to appear as the list evolves and gets shared. Below is just a small selection of organizations you may want to check out.

Black Girls Run
www.blackgirlsrun.com

Big City Mountaineers
www.bigcitymountaineers.org

Brothers of Climbing
www.boccrew.com

Brown Girls Climb
www.browngirlsclimb.com

Center for Diversity & the Environment
www.cdeinspires.org

Children & Nature Network
www.childrenandnature.org

Climbers of Color
www.climbersofcolor.org

Color in the Outdoors
www.colorintheoutdoors.org

Color the Wasatch
Affiliated with the American Alpine Club
www.patelp.com/color-the-wasatch.html

Cruxing in Color
www.cruxingincolor.com

Environmental Learning for Kids
www.elkkids.org

GirlTrek
www.girltrek.org

Green Latinos
www.greenlatinos.org

Green Muslims
www.greenmuslims.org

Greening Youth Foundation
gyfoundation.org

Groundwork USA
groundworkusa.org

Hispanic Access Foundation
hispanicaccess.org

Indigenous Women Hike
www.facebook.com/indigenouswomenhike

Inspiring Connections Outdoors (ICO)
Affiliated with the Sierra Club
www.sierraclub.org/ico

Kween Werk
www.kweenwerk.com

Latino Outdoors
www.latinooutdoors.org

LATINXHIKERS
www.instagram.com/latinxhikers

Melanin Base Camp
www.melaninbasecamp.com

The Mountaineers
www.mountaineers.org

National Outdoor Leadership School (NOLS)
www.nols.edu

Native Women's Wilderness
www.nativewomenswilderness.org

NatureBridge
naturebridge.org

Outdoor Afro
www.outdoorafro.com

Outdoor Outreach
www.outdooroutreach.org

Outward Bound
www.outwardbound.org

Society for Advancement of Chicanos/Hispanics and Native Americans in Science (SACNAS)
www.sacnas.org

Soul Trak Outdoors
soultrak.com

Student Conservation Association
www.thesca.org

Vibe Tribe Adventures
www.vibetribeadventures.org

Wild Diversity
wilddiversity.com

Wilderness Inquiry
www.wildernessinquiry.org

RECOMMENDED READING

Many authors in the BIPOC community have contributed to the exploration of our relationship with the natural environment. I am grateful to call a few of them my friends. Several have appeared as guests on my monthly book group and YouTube series "The Joy Trip Reading Project."

Books

Carter, Majora. *Reclaiming Your Community: You Don't Have to Move Out of Your Neighborhood to Live in a Better One.* Oakland, CA: Berrett-Koehler, 2022.

Désir, Alison Mariella. *Running While Black: Finding Freedom in a Sport That Wasn't Built for Us.* New York: Portfolio, 2022.

Edmondson, Dudley. *The Black & Brown Faces in America's Wildest Places: African Americans Making Nature and the Environment a Part of Their Everyday Lives.* Cambridge, MN: Adventure Publications, 2006.

Finney, Carolyn. *Black Faces, White Spaces: Reimagining the Relationship of African Americans to the Great Outdoors.* Chapel Hill: University of North Carolina Press, 2014.

Flowers, Catherine Coleman. *Waste: One Woman's Fight Against America's Dirty Secret.* New York: The New Press, 2020.

Harris, Eddy L. *South of Haunted Dreams: A Memoir.* New York: Henry Holt, 1997.

Harris, J. R. *Way Out There: Adventures of a Wilderness Trekker.* Seattle: Mountaineers Books, 2017.

Henson, Matthew. *A Negro Explorer at the North Pole: The Autobiography of Matthew Henson.* Montpelier, VT: Invisible Cities Press, 2001.

Johnson, Shelton. *Gloryland.* San Francisco: Sierra Club Books, 2009.

Kyu, Dave, and Ilyssa Kyu, eds. *Campfire Stories, Volume II: Tales from America's National Parks and Trails.* Seattle: Mountaineers Books, 2023.

Lanham, J. Drew. *The Home Place: Memoirs of a Colored Man's Love Affair with Nature.* Minneapolis: Milkweed Editions, 2017.

Mapp, Rue. *Nature Swagger: Stories and Visions of Black Joy in the Outdoors.* San Francisco: Chronicle Books, 2022.

McDonald, Bernadette. *Alpine Rising: Sherpas, Baltis, and the Triumph of Local Climbers in the Greater Ranges.* Seattle: Mountaineers Books, 2024.

Penniman, Leah. *Black Earth Wisdom: Soulful Conversations with Black Environmentalists.* New York: Amistad/HarperCollins, 2023.

Savoy, Lauret Edith. *Trace: Memory, History Race, and the American Landscape.* Berkeley, CA: Counterpoint Press, 2015.

Stawski, Jeannette. *The Outdoor Leader: Resilience, Integrity, and Adventure.* Seattle: Mountaineers Books, 2024.

Wendler, Amber, and Shaz Zamore, eds. *Been Outside: Adventures of Black Women, Nonbinary, and Gender Nonconforming People in Nature.* Seattle: Mountaineers Books, 2023.

Online Articles

Abrams, Jonathan. "Meet the Ebony Anglers, Five Black Women Catching Fish and Stares." *New York Times*, November 1, 2020. www.nytimes.com/2020/11/01/sports/ebony-anglers-fishing-black-women.html.

American Trails. "Historical Perspectives on Racism in the Outdoors and Looking Forward." June 2020. www.americantrails.org/resources/the-arch-of-history-is-long-but-it-bends-towards-justice.

Conniff, Richard. "How a Notorious Racist Inspired America's National Parks." *Mother Jones*, July/August 2016. www.motherjones.com/environment/2016/07/anniversary-national-parks-racist-history-madison-grant/.

Mills, James Edward. "Bringing Black History to Life in the Great Outdoors." *New York Times*, September 20, 2021. www.nytimes.com/interactive/2021/09/20/multimedia/black-national-park-rangers.html.

———. "Here's How National Parks Are Working to Fight Racism." National Geographic, June 23, 2020. www.nationalgeographic.com/travel/national-parks/article/more-diversity-how-to-make-national-parks-anti-racist.

———. "In Michigan, Making the Outdoors More Accessible to People of Color." National Geographic, June 10, 2021. www.nationalgeographic.com/travel/article/in-michigan-making-the-outdoors-more-accessible-to-people-of-color.

———. "These People of Color Transformed US National Parks," National Geographic, August 5, 2020. www.nationalgeographic.com/travel/article/people-of-color-who-transformed-us-national-parks.

Mock, Brentin. "Want to Attract a New Generation to the National Parks? Find a Few New Rangers." Grist, March 28, 2014. grist.org/climate-energy/want-to-attract-a-new-generation-to-the-national-parks-find-a-few-new-rangers/.

Noor, Poppy. "Being Black While in Nature: You're An Endangered Species." *Guardian*, May 31, 2020. www.theguardian.com/lifeandstyle/2020/may/31/being-black-while-in-nature-youre-an-endangered-species.

Walker, Joshua. "Lions and Tigers and Black Folk, Oh My! Why Black People Should Take Up Space in the Outdoors." Melanin Base Camp, April 11, 2019. www.melaninbasecamp.com/around-the-bonfire/2019/4/10/why-black-people-should-take-up-space-outdoors.

Williams, Danielle. "The Melanin Base Camp Guide to Allyship." Melanin Base Camp, July 7, 2019. www.melaninbasecamp.com/trip-reports/2019/7/7/mbc-guide-to-outdoor-allyship.

Willingham, A. J. "These Black Nature Lovers Are Busting Stereotypes, One Cool Bird at a Time." CNN, June 3, 2020. www.cnn.com/2020/06/03/us/black-birders-week-black-in-stem-christian-cooper-scn-trnd/index.html.

The Adventure Gap: A Reader's Guide

Since this book by James Edward Mills was first published in 2014, it has been used in classrooms around the country, as well as by individual readers, to inspire discussion and debate on topics related to diversity, equity, and inclusion in the outdoors. Here, the author and publisher share some sample questions and topics related to events and characters in the book to help readers further explore these issues in their own conversations.

How do you define your place in nature? Do you feel welcome there, that you belong? Some people describe their time outside as "happy," "peaceful," "expectant," "nervous," "excited," among others. What adjectives might you use to describe your own time in natural settings?

When you go outside, what role do you play? Are you actively recreating or more passively enjoying? Do you take the lead in heading outdoors or do you follow others outside?

Before reading this book, did you experience or observe examples of "the adventure gap" in your own outdoor excursions? What did that look and feel like?

Can just a single journey or adventure, such as that of Expedition Denali, inspire real change? If so, how? What does that change look like to you?

Does the fact that the Expedition Denali team didn't actually summit the mountain matter to you? What lessons can we learn about the journey, even though they didn't arrive at their desired destination?

When the Expedition Denali team reaches the plateau known as the "Football Field" (at 19,620'), they can see the summit ridge and climbers heading to the top. Yet there are also darkening skies, thunder, and snow flurries. Mills writes,

> Their goal was in sight and within reach, but everyone around them was suddenly in a mad scramble to head in the opposite direction. . . . before confusion could turn to panic, Aaron took control of the situation. In a brilliant gesture of leadership, he turned to the group and spread his arms wide with his back to the mountain and the storm. He smiled broadly and declared loudly over the sound of the thunder: "Everybody, we're at 19,620 feet. Congratulations and welcome to your high point! It's time to start heading down."

Why does Mills describe Aaron's actions as "a brilliant gesture of leadership"? Do you agree?

Who of the expedition members did you find most inspiring as you read? Why? In the new "Where Are They Now" section, did your interest remain the same or pivot to a different person?

Intersecting the story of Expedition Denali, Mills profiles six other athletes from different eras and sports but all people of color. Why do you think it was important to include these additional stories?

It wasn't until 2015, two years after Expedition Denali's summit attempt in 2013, that the mountain formerly known as Mount McKinley had its name legally changed to the Indigenous word Denali, meaning "the high one" or "the tall one" in Athabascan. How does this relate to the events in this book, if at all?

Early in the book, Mills writes,

> There is a link between recreating in the outdoors and wanting to protect it. People who spend time outdoors have the opportunity to appreciate its beauty and importance. Individuals across the nation and around the world who recognize the benefits of having access to fresh air, clean water, and open green space for their health and well-being will devote time and money to preserve those qualities. Having created loyal and long-standing relationships with the places they love most, they will pass their affection down to their children, establishing a legacy of stewardship that spans generations.

Mills then goes on to discuss some of the challenges, particularly for people of color, to spending time outdoors, including lack of access, high costs of participation, historic discrimination in outdoor spaces, and other factors that create "the adventure gap." How does the story of a group of Black climbers attempting to summit a mountain relate to conservation and stewardship? Do you think this is the core meaning of the book?

Do you personally feel a sense of obligation to protect the natural world for the long term? If not just for yourself, what about for others?

In the New Afterword, Mills touches on the intersection of the outdoors, recreation, and conservation movements with that of social justice. How do you see these areas relating? What actions do you think the outdoor industry still needs to pursue in order to achieve more equitable interest and access?

Have you observed or experienced progress in your own outdoors community, in terms of diversity and inclusion, since this book was first published in 2014? Has anything changed—for better or for worse?

Being in the mountains and climbing high peaks represents just one path in outdoor recreation. What are other outdoor adventures, activities, and/or places that inspire you? Do you have any specific goals you hope to achieve in the natural world?

Index

About the Author

EVAN GREEN

JAMES EDWARD MILLS is a National Geographic Explorer as well as a contributor to *National Geographic* magazine. He is a Fellow of the Mountain & Wilderness Writing Program of the Banff Centre in Alberta, Canada, and a recipient of the Paul K. Petzoldt Award for Environmental Education and the H. Adams Carter Literary Award from the American Alpine Club. His writings and photography have appeared in various publications including *Outside*, *Rock & Ice*, *Alpinist*, *The Clymb*, *Appalachia Journal*, *The Guardian*, *The New York Times*, *Sierra*, *Land & People*, and History.com. As a Fellow at the University of Wisconsin Nelson Institute for Environmental Studies and an adjunct lecturer at Western Colorado University, Mills teaches a course called "Outdoors for All" on diversity, equity, and inclusion in outdoor recreation and public land management. Mills lives in Madison, Wisconsin, with his wife, Shamane, and two lovable dogs, Mikala and Sasha. Learn more at www.joytripproject.com.

OTHER TITLES YOU MIGHT ENJOY

The Outdoor Leader: Resilience, Integrity, and Adventure
Jeannette Stawski
Essential attributes of outdoor leadership, featuring stories and advice from a diverse range of outdoor professionals

Campfire Stories: Volumes I and II
Tales from America's National Parks and Trails
Edited by Dave Kyu and Ilyssa Kyu
Stories, poems, and more about 11 national parks and 2 national trails from an engaging and diverse collection of writers

Been Outside: Adventures of Black Women, Nonbinary, and Gender Nonconforming People in Nature
Edited by Amber Wendler and Shaz Zamore
From Black natural scientists and outdoor professionals, inspiring stories of acceptance through nature

Crossing Denali: An Ordinary Man's Adventure Atop North America
Michael Fenner
A thrilling story of adventure and survival!

The Bond: Survival on Denali and Mount Huntington
Simon McCartney
Winner of Banff and Boardman Tasker book awards

www.mountaineersbooks.org